THE NEW ZEALANDERS
HOW THEY LIVE AND WORK

The New Zealanders

HOW THEY LIVE AND WORK

R. J. Johnston

DAVID & CHARLES
NEWTON ABBOT LONDON
NORTH POMFRET (VT) VANCOUVER

for
Christopher and Lucy

ISBN 0 7153 7170 3

© R. J. Johnston 1976

First published 1976
Second impression 1977

Printed in Great Britain by
REDWOOD BURN LIMITED
Trowbridge & Esher
for David & Charles (Publishers) Limited
Brunel House Newton Abbot Devon

Contents

5

6   *Contents*

List of Illustrations

General map of New Zealand: land over 1,000 feet is shaded

Introduction

NEW ZEALAND is located in that part of the globe which for a long time European cartographers represented as *Terra Australis Incognita*. The latter adjective is no longer strictly relevant, but although the majority of New Zealanders are of recent British stock, there are many aspects of New Zealand which are unknown to northern hemisphere residents. Certain facts are widely known, of course, many of them about either sheep or sport, and various myths and half-truths circulate, about the indigenous Maori population, for example, and also about the weather. Most of these 'facts' and 'myths' appear to be favourable towards New Zealand, for an excellent indicator of either economic ills or bad winters in Britain seems to be a lengthening of the queues of would-be emigrants at London's New Zealand House.

Visitors often write about overseas countries they have been to. Often they are critical, especially if they have spent only a short time as a visitor and have done little else than make superficial comparisons, either with their homeland or with some Utopian preconception. New Zealand has suffered its share of such volumes and articles, as well as the similar comments of disgruntled migrants. But hopefully the present book does not fit into that category. It is an attempt to portray, after seven-and-a-half years' residence and work among New Zealanders, the major features of the society that has been fashioned in the south-west Pacific, using the framework of the *How They Live and Work* series.

One somewhat sceptical commentator has described New Zealand's social system as 'comfortable but mediocre materialism'. And there is more than a grain of truth in that statement.

9

Material standards are indeed high; what is more, they are widely spread. And, because the country has but three million people and is isolated from the main social, political, and economic currents of the world, it is not surprising that New Zealand lacks the cosmopolitan initiative of other countries. To counter this, however, its peoples have ensured that very few of their number suffer the indignities imposed on sizeable proportions of the populations in so-called more 'advanced' societies. And so, with high general material standards, New Zealand is a comfortable place. In times of economic plenty, it is secure in its comfort; in times of economic ills, as now, the security can so easily be breached, and few English-speaking countries will have endured such widespread suffering as was the lot of the one-and-a-half million New Zealanders in the 1930s. External economic forces are today very threatening to that cosy, egalitarian materialism which generations have forged out of the ruins of the 1930s, and New Zealanders are ever active in their search for means to continue their prosperity. Within their country, too, they face problems which might upset the social order, created by urbanisation and industrialisation, by regional disparities in welfare levels, and by the need to integrate Polynesian and European elements into a truly multi-racial society.

The 1970s are a decade of rapid change, whose rate seems to be ever-increasing. Most of this book was written in mid-1974, so that by the time it is published a number of its 'facts' will undoubtedly be obsolete. To avoid a superfluity of these, monetary values have been quoted sparingly, because of the probable effects of internal inflation and external exchange rate shifts. At the time of writing, $1.00 NZ was worth about £0.51 UK and $1.33 US.

I

The Country and the People

Around the Pacific Ocean is a belt characterised by frequent earthquakes, occasional volcanic eruptions, many extinct and dormant volcanoes, and other evidence of seismic activity such as hot springs and geysers. One portion of the south-western quadrant of this pan-Pacific girdle is occupied by New Zealand, comprising two large islands and a myriad small ones. Together, these cover some 269,000 square kilometres, about the same area as that of Great Britain, three-quarters that of Japan, and only three per cent of the extent of the conterminous United States. Unlike Britain and Japan, however, New Zealand is the home of only just over three million people, so that despite similarities in size, and also latitudinal location, the contrasts between the northern and southern hemisphere island groups are many.

THE PHYSICAL ENVIRONMENT

Geologically, New Zealand is a young country, most of its present shape resulting from relatively recent mountain-building activity. Tectonic forces raised a spine of ranges that forms the country's major axis, with only one major breach in the narrow stretch of turbulent water (Cook Strait) which separates the two main islands. The sedimentary rocks of this elongated land mass are susceptible to erosion, so that the landscape is deeply etched and corrugated. Together with their height, this has made the mountain ranges a formidable barrier to human endeavour and given them a pervasive influence over the development of local societies.

11

The South Island contains the country's highest mountains, part of an unbroken chain extending from the fjords of the south-west, with their steep, imposing walls rising sheer from the sea, to the more finely-dissected drowned valleys of the Marlborough Sounds in the north-east. Approximately midway along this axis are the highest peaks, culminating in Mt Cook (3,763m)—Aorangi, 'the great cloud piercer' of Maori legend. From the ranges, large rivers tumble swiftly to the sea; few are very long, especially those on the west coast, but they carry immense volumes of water and may swell to enormous proportions in times of heavy rain and snow melt. Their passages through the ranges are almost invariably tortuous, particularly on the eastern flanks where rivers pass alternately through deep narrow gorges and open inland basins. Beyond the main mountain ranges are blocks of younger, lower hill country (often termed downlands). And finally there is a series of coastal plains, mostly small in both length and breadth (the main exception is the large triangle of the Canterbury Plains) and separated from each other either by downland blocks or by isolated products of periods of volcanic activity.

The mountain chain in the North Island is much lower, though still intricately dissected and very difficult to penetrate, let alone traverse. It is breached in only one place—the Manawatu Gorge immediately east of Palmerston North—but is clearly subdividable into a number of separate, equally wild and obstructive, ranges. From the northern shores of Cook Strait, these continue the south-south-west/north-north-east grain of the South Island, separating the small flood plains (such as Poverty Bay and Hawke's Bay), and inland basins (notably the Wairarapa), with their attendant encircling lower, easily-eroded hill country, from the bulk of the island.

To the west of the main ranges is a geologically more complex area, forming the arm, oriented to the north-north-west, which gives the island its characteristic Y shape. The central portion of the land mass is a plateau of extruded volcanic materials, capped by the active cones of Mts Ruapehu (2,797m) and Ngauruhoe (2,290m), and the neighbouring extinct peak of Tongariro (1,968m). North of these is the main area of current thermal activity, extending north from the caldera of Lake

Taupo, through Rotorua—famed for its bubbling mudpools, hot springs, and geysers—and the Bay of Plenty to the active volcano of White Island. A salient of this active volcanic area extends through the Northland peninsula. The Auckland isthmus, population focus for separate racial majorities, is dotted with small conical hills, providing variety to the urban scene as well as useful raw materials for various construction work.

Apart from the volcanic areas, that portion of the North Island west of the main ranges is characterised by ranges of deeply dissected hill country. There are few extensive areas of flat land, the main exception being in the valley of the Waikato river, New Zealand's longest at 425 kilometres. Extensions of the volcanic regions form enclaves in this country, however, most notably the almost perfect cone of Taranaki's Mt Egmont (2,517m), which vies with Mt Cook as the New Zealand mountain emblem.

Seismic activity continues, in the geothermal activity of Rotorua and elsewhere, the occasional emissions from Ngauruhoe and Ruapehu, and the average of about a hundred earthquakes recorded each year. No part of the country is completely immune from quakes, though they are concentrated along the fault lines of the main mountain chains. Most are slight, and leave little evidence of their action; some, indeed, are hardly felt. But a few are destructive and cause extensive landscape changes. Christchurch's Anglican Cathedral has twice lost the top of its spire, and some of Wellington's streets, including the only road linking it to the rest of the North Island, follow recently uplifted terraces. The most devastating earthquake in living memory centred on Napier in 1931, with the harbour and lagoon being raised above sea level—7,500 acres of new land were formed—and the loss of 256 lives. Volcanic activity, too, may severely affect human occupancy. The release of water from a lake temporarily dammed by volcanic ejectamenta, swept away a railway bridge on Christmas Eve, 1953, killing 151 passengers on a train which was on the bridge at the moment of impact.

New Zealand is a rugged country, therefore, characterised by difficult mountain and hill terrain. Indeed, much of the two main islands is made up of such landscapes, especially the larger South Island, as shown by the following table, compiled by Cumberland and Fox.

Percentage of the land area which is:	North Island	South Island	New Zealand
Mountain	18	70	49
Steep and Broken Hill Country	45	12	25
Downland and Easy Hill Country	26	9	15
Plateaux	5	0	3
Plain	6	9	8

New Zealand is the southern hemisphere antipodes of France and Spain, and its latitudinal extent is similar to that of California and the original thirteen colonies of the United States. But its climate differs from those of its northern hemisphere counterparts because of its mid-oceanic, rather than continental fringe, location. As the country is bisected by the 40° south line of latitude, its climate is dominated by the eastward passage of successions of depressions and anti-cyclones. The latter generally pass to the north of the country; many of the depressions only skirt New Zealand to the south, and their main contribution is the rainfall brought by the cold fronts. These usually traverse the two islands from south-south-west to north-north-east.

The confrontation of these weather systems with the mountain backbone provides the main features in the spatial variability of weather and climate. Rainfall is plentiful on the west coasts, especially of the South Island where the mountains are high and but a few kilometres from the sea. Hokitika receives 2,895mm in an average year—much of it at night and in heavy falls, so its sunshine average is 5·3 hours per day. The far south of the island is also damp—1,021mm at Invercargill annually on average—but the north-east, in the alpine rainshadow and reached by the northwards-moving fronts only after they have deposited much of their moisture, is extremely dry and sunny—Blenheim averages 6·7 hours of sunshine daily over the year. Rainshadow areas of the east coast are also dry and sunny, notably the Canterbury Plains and the inland basins of Central Otago: the latter are semi-desertlike in character, with Alexandra averaging only 342mm of rain each year.

As well as being the tail-end recipient of moisture-bearing weather systems proceeding from the south, the North Island is also affected by sequences originating to its north-west. Tropical depressions move along the Queensland coast and then head south-eastwards across the Tasman Sea towards Northland, bringing rain, particularly in late summer and autumn. As a result the North Island is generally the wetter, especially in the winter months—Auckland's annual average rainfall is 1,263mm —and seasonal drought is rarer there than in the South Island. Occasionally the tropical depressions continue south across the island as intense cyclones, with extremely strong winds and torrential rainfall. The most memorable recent such storm was at Easter 1968, during which the inter-island ferry *Wahine* sank in Wellington Harbour with the loss of 52 lives.

There is a latitudinal extent of some fourteen degrees over the two main islands, which produces a clear north-south gradation in temperatures, especially in winter when the South Island is frequently affected by air moving from the Antarctic. The average daily temperature maxima and minima for summer (January) and winter (July), in degrees celsius, at the four main cities are:

	Summer		Winter	
	Maxima	*Minima*	*Maxima*	*Minima*
Auckland	23	16	14	8
Wellington	20	13	11	5
Christchurch	22	12	10	1
Dunedin	19	11	10	3

There is also marked variation in frost frequencies, which are most common and severe—outside the mountains—in the rain-shadow areas of the eastern South Island. Central Otago averages some 150 frosts a year and Christchurch 89; because most of these occur during anti-cyclonic conditions, the early morning frost and fog is usually followed by a still, sunny day.

Extremes of climate are in the mountains; on the coastal plains, where most New Zealanders live, the sea has a strong moderating effect. The far north of the North Island, and also the west coast of the South Island, is much warmer in winter, and generally more humid. Most of the country is windy,

Wellington notoriously so, and folklore has it that a Wellington resident can always be identified because he puts his hands to his hat on rounding every corner. Canterbury has a characteristic wind, the nor'wester, which is most frequent in spring and has the warm, dry characteristics typical of other föhn winds such as the Chinook and Mistral. But the main feature everywhere is the changeability of the weather. Long periods of any particular type are rare: storms may be intense and rainfall heavy, but in a day or so it will undoubtedly be bright and sunny again.

New Zealand's surface features are products of combinations of geology, topography and climate. The generally ample rainfall and year-round equable temperatures, for example, allowed the development of luxuriant, dark, evergreen forest cover over much of the land surface. Only the dry eastern plains—notably Canterbury and the inland basins behind it—and the higher mountain ranges had a 'natural' grassland cover. This was a tussock grassland, notable still for its clumps of larger plants. Floral abundance was not matched in the fauna, however, because of the islands' isolation from major source areas. There are, for example, no native snakes and, until the Polynesian migrations, there was only one mammal—a bat. The most distinctive indigenes are the birds, particularly the flightless varieties such as the rare nocturnal kiwi and the large moa, which was hunted to extinction on the plains. Notable also is the tuatara, a nocturnal reptile of a type which became extinct on other continents about a hundred million years ago.

In many areas, landscape details reflect the colder eras of the Pleistocene ice ages. An extensive system of valley glaciers was focused on the South Island's high mountains; an ice-cap may have existed in the far south-west. Deep glacial troughs were gouged; on the western mountain flanks, these were later flooded by the sea to form the deep inlets of Fiordland whereas on the eastern side, long deep lakes, many dammed by morainic deposits, fill the troughs and add much to the area's scenic splendour. Glacial activity in the North Island was restricted to the highest peaks, and today there are no remnant small glaciers, though one disappeared only recently from the slopes of Ruapehu. A number of valley glaciers are found in the alpine valleys of the South Island; the most remarkable being the Fox and Franz Jozef glaciers which flow down the western flank of the Mt Cook massif, to within a few metres of sea level and a few kilometres from the Tasman Sea. Their snouts occasionally abut on to sub-tropical forested slopes, presenting a vivid landscape contrast.

The coastal plains have been formed of detritus carried down from the mountains by rivers. Some are covered by rich alluvial soils; others are stony and thinly mantled, but may be important water reservoirs. River beds are often wide, with the stream itself flowing through a maze of braided channels occupying only a small part of the total area. Most of the rivers, in both the mountain and plains segments of their courses, are inset within suites of well-defined terraces, marking climatic and sea-level oscillations during the landscape-building process.

FIRST SETTLERS

When humans first arrived in New Zealand is not known, for the Maori have no recorded history and their language had no written form until the Europeans arrived. Most of what is known about Polynesian colonisation of Aotearoa—'the land of the long white cloud'—is thus shrouded in the mists of oral tradition. Methods of dating archaeological remains suggest a Polynesian occupancy stretching back at least a thousand years, but there is intense academic controversy about the nature of the colonisation and whether it can be divided into several clear phases.

How the Maori arrived in Aotearoa is also unknown. Many scholars support the thesis that discovery and colonisation were accidental, a consequence of drift voyages of a thousand miles or more, at the whim of current and wind. But others claim that the diversion of intended short journeys by nature's caprices would not have brought kinship groups with the flora and fauna that they used in their colonisation. Thus these writers claim that the migrations were intentional. But did the Maori set out from their ancestral home of Hawaiki seeking Aotearoa? And did the first discoverers return and spread the news to more potential migrants? Maori legend tells only that the original settlers came in a fleet of large outrigger canoes; to each of which tribal ancestries are still traced. European translation of such a legend is fraught with difficulty, however. The Maori came from eastern Polynesia more than a thousand years ago, by methods and for reasons unknown. Whether there was a long period of continual sailings, sporadic settlement booms, or merely a single great movement has not been, and probably never will be, established.

Their new land, albeit a temperate and fertile one, was very different from the Maori's previous home. The flora and fauna offered few opportunities for hunting and gathering, though tribes clearly survived on the South Island plains by hunting the moa, and by fishing. Indeed, the birds, fish, and shellfish offered a good protein diet, which was fortified by eating the introduced kumara (sweet potato). The fish diet provided protein to counter an iodine deficiency which was a catalyst for goitre, widespread among the Maori. (Today, all packaged salt is iodised.) The bulk of the population lived in the northern North Island, particularly on the coasts, where forests were plentiful in building timber and the native flax provided a material for fibre and cloth. Groups moved throughout both islands, however, establishing settlements where they halted to exploit local resources. Subsistence agriculture was the basic occupation, but there was some trading in both surplus foods and the prized greenstone, from the South Island's west coast, which was used for clubs and ornaments.

The Maori's was a tribal society, based on kinship and the possession of territory. Within it, status was based on ancestry, with the chieftains and cultural leaders being those with traceable links to tribal ancestors. Individual and family rights were few; most items, in particular land, were communally owned. Tribes were divided into groups (*hapus*) which lived semi-independent existences in nucleated settlements focused on the open *marae* (communal meeting place) and elaborately carved meeting-house. Conflicts between adjacent groups, often precipitated by food shortages, were frequent; at such times, groups would retreat into fortified villages (*pas*) which were

usually stockaded and surrounded by complex defensive earth-
works. Territorial readjustments may have resulted from such
conflicts; long-distance migrations were imposed on the vanquished in some cases.

THE PAKEHA ARRIVAL

As many as 250,000 Maoris may have been living in Aotearoa
in the late eighteenth century, when *pakeha* settlement of their
land began. (Pakeha is Maori for 'foreigner' and is now
applied to all white men; maori itself means 'normal'.) The
first pakeha visitors came in 1642; Abel Tasman visited the
western coasts, but lost four men in a skirmish with the natives
close to what is now Takaka. Initiation of the contacts which
led to British sovereignty over the islands was in 1769, with the
initial visit of Captain James Cook, whose first landfall was near
to the present city of Gisborne.

New Zealand provided Cook with bases for his later voyages
of discovery, on which he charted the coastline and collected
scientific data, meanwhile establishing reasonably cordial contacts with the inhabitants. The information he took back to
England precipitated other expeditions to the new lands—by
several French as well as British sailors, who were followed by
traders seeking timber and flax, whales and seals. Much of the
early commerce was with Sydney; its New Zealand focus was
in the Bay of Islands, on the Northland east coast. Here the first
missionary preached in 1814, and in 1840 the country was
ceded to Britain, with the initial 'capital' established at
Russell.

The early pakeha settlements were lawless places, but the
British government was reluctant to impose its rule upon them.
Eventually it yielded to pressure from residents, and established
the colony with a party of civil servants despatched from New
South Wales. A meeting of Maori chiefs agreed to invite
British authority, and on 6 February 1840 signed the never-
ratified Treaty of Waitangi, by which they ceded their
sovereignty to Queen Victoria in return for full rights as
British subjects plus retention of control of their land and other

resources. Other chiefs signed later, and the formal British takeover was on 21 May.

Several of the important initial settlements were established by the New Zealand Company, set up in London to execute Edward Gibbon Wakefield's theories of colonisation. Four bridgeheads were established, at Nelson, New Plymouth, Wanganui, and Wellington; these were followed a few years later by similar settlements, at Dunedin established by the Free Presbyterian Otago Association and at Christchurch by the Anglican Canterbury Association. Meanwhile Auckland became the new country's capital, and the only 'unplanned' town of that early period. Wakefield's theories involved the transplanting of English rural, hierarchical society, based on land ownership, to New Zealand. Early years were difficult for the settlers, however, as the system of land tenure was designed for an agricultural economy which was unsuited to an environment in which pastoralism soon prevailed.

HISTORICAL LANDMARKS

Most rapid development by pakeha settlers occurred in the South Island during the first few decades after the Treaty of Waitangi. The fertile grasslands of the Canterbury Plains, for example, were used to graze Merino sheep imported from Australia, and the city of Christchurch prospered accordingly. A massive boost to the island's economy was given in the 1860s by the discovery of gold deposits, in Central Otago in 1861 and Westland in 1863. A great rush of miners, many from Australia and California, trebled the South Island population to 160,000 by the end of the decade, and Dunedin became the country's major city and commercial centre. Then, as the boom faded, many of the miners moved on to the land, opening up thousands of hectares for farming: the later decades of the century saw a 'wheat bonanza' on the eastern plains.

North Island development was hampered in the first years of the colony by two considerations, the almost impenetrable native forest ('the bush') and the competing land claims of Maori and pakeha. The latter rivalry climaxed in a series of

Maori Wars during the 1860s, in which several thousand British troops were used to defeat, with considerable difficulty, the poorly-equipped natives. The vanquished then retreated, into the heart of the island (the King Country, so-called because it was the locus of a separatist movement) and the remote fastnesses of Northland and the East Cape, leaving the pakeha with the better land.

Early agriculture was limited in its scope by what it could successfully convey to the distant Australian, let alone British, markets, and the main export was wool. An innovation of 1882 revolutionised the face of much of New Zealand, however. The refrigerated ship's hold meant that sheep-meat could be successfully preserved for sale in a country 12,000 miles away. British capital was used to build meat-freezing works along the coasts of both islands, and also to finance the opening-up of large tracts of country, in which sheep were raised as multi-purpose animals. Refrigeration was also the catalyst for dairy farming, supporting local co-operative factories which manufactured butter and cheese for Britain. This type of farming was most suited to the damper North Island, and the bush was rapidly burned and felled, to be replaced by pastures of imported grasses.

As the farming frontier pushed the bush back, so the North Island came to dominate the country's economy, which itself changed very little in the next fifty years. In 1900, the two islands were almost equal in population numbers; today, about three-quarters of the 'Kiwis' are North Islanders. The farm production of butter and cheese, meat and wool was remitted to the 'mother country' from which a wide range of manufactured goods was purchased in return. This specialisation and dependence made New Zealand extremely vulnerable to the vicissitudes of the world economic situation, and she suffered greatly during the depression of the 1930s. Greater industrial self-sufficiency was only really sought after 1945, however, as the population grew sufficiently large to support a range of factory types, and the 1960s heralded a drive towards a more diversified economy, as a consequence of Britain's clearly-stated European intentions.

Just as Britain was loath to annex New Zealand, so the

country she eventually formed was reluctant to leave the colonial fold. Responsible government was granted in 1856, giving control over all internal matters—except Maori affairs, which remained for a few years with the Governor-General—to an elected parliament. In 1900, the decision was made not to join the emerging Australian federation; in 1915, however, a joint venture with Australia—the Gallipoli landings by the ANZAC force—was an event from which many people date New Zealand's (and Australia's) achievement of nationhood. New Zealand became a dominion in 1907, but the British tie remained strong, despite friction over local inability to conclude commercial treaties and the infant nation's insistence on taking its place at Versailles in 1919. Independence was formally realised by the 1931 Statute of Westminster—though parliament in Wellington did not ratify this until 1947.

Perhaps, above all else, it was the Second World War which led to altered New Zealand attitudes towards the country still frequently referred to as 'home'. Though devoted in their rallying to the British cause, the Pacific islanders came to realise that Britain, notably Britain's navy, could not protect them and that the United States—as it proved in the decisive Battle of the Coral Sea—could. Legal and regal ties with Britain have been maintained, therefore, but New Zealand has sought new friends, allies, and trading partners. In 1966, troops were sent to Vietnam; in the 1970s, leadership of the many small nations of the South Pacific has been actively sought, along with increasing independence of thought in foreign policy; in 1974, the first New Zealand Day was celebrated (on 6 February), and Queen Elizabeth's official title was changed to 'Queen of New Zealand'.

POPULATION

New Zealand presently has just over three million inhabitants, a fraction under one-tenth of whom are Maori. The quarter of a million members of the Maori race may be fewer than were in Aotearoa at the time of Cook's arrival, but as the definition of a Maori is one who claims membership of that race, and as there has been considerable Maori-pakeha mixture, the number of people with some indigenous ancestry is undoubtedly understated. In recent decades, there has been a dramatic Maori demographic resurgence. After the 1860s wars, defeated and demoralised, and ravaged by pakeha disease and booze, they were thought to be a dying race: extinction indeed seemed likely, for by 1896 they numbered only 42,000. Since then, and especially from the 1920s on, they have been aided by modern medicine, and, with the guidance of able politicians such as Ngata, the native culture has been rejuvenated. For several decades, the Maori birth rate has been among the world's highest; today nearly sixty per cent of Maori are aged under twenty, compared with thirty-five per cent of pakeha in this age group.

Apart from the brief mining interludes, Europeans came to New Zealand in the nineteenth century mostly as agriculturalists and pastoralists. But although the country's main title to wealth has been its grass, once this was established a large labour force was not needed to extract the fruits of its fertility. There was a much greater demand for merchants and bankers, artisans and clerks, dockers and shopkeepers, than for farmers and rural labourers. So very soon the towns, most of them ports, became dominant in the population distribution, and four of these places became established as the nation's main urban areas.

The two largest urban areas are in the North Island, which is dominated by Auckland's 630,000 residents. The country's main port and industrial centre, Auckland has doubled its population in the last twenty-five years. Its prosperity is based on its large and fertile hinterland, in contrast to Wellington, which serves a small, rugged, and much poorer tributary area. This latter city has been the capital for a very centralised society since 1865, and it now houses over 300,000 people in its extensive, discontinuous conurbation. In the South Island, almost 280,000 of the 810,000 inhabitants live in the plains city of Christchurch, nestled under the extinct volcanoes of Banks Peninsula. A further 110,000 live in Dunedin, now but a shadow of its mid-nineteenth-century commercial glory and rapidly declining in relative size and importance.

After the 'four main centres', as they are commonly known, comes a group of provincial cities, most of which act as service centres for one of the pockets of fertile coastal plain. Most are ports; most have populations of about 30,000. (From north to south they are Whangarei, Tauranga, Rotorua, Gisborne, New Plymouth, Wanganui, Masterton, Nelson and Timaru; only Wanganui is declining in population.) Their larger counterparts—Hamilton (81,000 people), Palmerston North (57,000), Invercargill (51,000) and the twin centres of Napier and Hastings (79,000)—play similar roles in the economy, acting as intermediaries between the farms and the 'four main centres'. Each of the cities in these lists also performs some unique economic function, however: at Whangarei, for example, is New Zealand's only oil refinery.

In all, about three-quarters of New Zealanders live in settlements with more than 1,000 residents, most of them in the urban areas already named. There is a range of smaller centres: some, as those on the South Island's west coast, serve small regions; others act as focal points for the more closely-settled districts, notably the dairying areas of Waikato and Taranaki. The remainder live in rural areas, mostly in dispersed farmsteads; farming in New Zealand does not generally support villages every few miles, as is so typical in much of Europe.

The Maori are also rapidly becoming an urban people, so that by 1971 half of them lived in one of the eighteen designated urban areas. As they became integrated into the pakeha economy, and their numbers rapidly grew, so their communally-held lands could not provide much more than a basic subsistence. So first the young men, and later whole families moved to the jobs and attractions of towns and cities. Since 1951, several of the remotest counties have suffered a literal decimation of their local population, especially its younger age groups. The main destination of the migrants has been Auckland, home now for nearly 50,000 Maori—four times as many as in the whole of the South Island. There, as in most cities, they live in what is generally the poorest housing and occupy the lowest-paid jobs, but deprivation is relative only, and, in absolute terms, especially compared with similar minority groups in the USA, Australia, and Britain, their conditions are excellent.

POPULATION CHARACTERISTICS

The vast majority of the non-Maori New Zealanders is of British stock, though in fact eighty-five per cent of them were born in New Zealand. All parts of Great Britain have contributed to the continual stream of immigrants; some, such as the Scots in Otago and Southland and the Irish in Westland and Southland, have made a clear and lasting impression on the districts in which they have settled, but in general the groups from various regions of the United Kingdom are undifferentiated in the 'Kiwi' population and landscape. One item of differentiation is in religious affiliation. Four main Christian denominations predominate: Anglican, with thirty-one per cent of the population claiming adherence, and Presbyterian, Roman Catholic, Methodist, with twenty, sixteen and six per cent respectively. In most parts of the country, these four groups are found in approximately those proportions. Southland and Otago, however, have Presbyterians outnumbering Anglicans by three to one and two to one respectively, and both Westland and Southland have Anglicans and Roman Catholics in almost equal numbers.

Small groups of immigrants have come from many other European countries. A number of these initiated their own settlements, but have since become totally assimilated and are almost indistinguishable. Germans, Scandinavians, and Dutch migrants typify this trend. Others have retained elements of their cultural, linguistic, and, sometimes, occupational separateness. Longest-settled inhabitants are the Yugoslavs: Dalmatian males originally came to the North Island to dig for gum in the kauri forests. They were later joined by other members of their families and formed several semi-independent settlements, notably some associated with vineyards around Auckland. More recent arrivals include Neapolitan Italians, and Greek, Polish, and Hungarian refugees. All of these have maintained their national identities in a variety of ways, but they form such a minute proportion of the population that most New Zealanders are hardly aware of their existence.

Finally, there are the non-European immigrants. Many Chinese males came during the 1860s goldrushes, but their permanent settlement was inhibited wherever possible and a continuous flow of families was prevented by legislation initiated to meet a general fear of the 'yellow peril'. A few remain, however, and today some 13,000 claim Chinese origins and race; many are market gardeners. There are also about 8,000 Indians.

More significant than the Asians in the contemporary scene are the recent arrivals from the Pacific islands. Many of them—from the Cook Islands, from Niue, and from the Tokelau Islands—have right of entry because of their New Zealand citizenship. The same was true for West Samoans until their country became independent in 1962; now they, like those from Tonga and Fiji, must obtain permits to enter either as workers or visitors. Most come for work—though many of them on visitor permits only—escaping at least temporarily from the problems of island subsistence economies, which they support by financial remittances. In number, there were only about 5,000 islanders in New Zealand twenty-five years ago; in 1971, there were at least 45,000. A majority is in Auckland—the home of 23,000 in 1971, excluding any born in New Zealand of immigrant parents; presently, there are more Niueans in Auckland than on their home island. Within Auckland, they live in close, 'village-like' settlements, adding to that city's cultural variety but often suffering—from Maori and pakeha alike—the indignities of racial prejudice and discrimination.

New Zealand is an attractive potential destination for would-be emigrants, both those from the Pacific islands drawn to the chances of jobs and money and those who seek to avoid the economic and social problems perceived in their homeland by many Britons. In the last few years, this has created a number of problems for their adopted country. Local manufacturing and service industries, notably the construction industry, have been unable to provide for the new residents, producing an inflationary situation. And many of the islanders, working illegally on visitor permits, have suffered exploitation, by employers and landlords alike, because of their position. As a counter, New Zealand rewrote its immigration policy in 1974.

There is now an annual quota for all migrants, and British (United Kingdom) passport holders no longer have a right of entry; all potential immigrants require an entry permit. The quota is based not on numbers alone but on needed work skills and ability to assimilate.

LANDSCAPES

The several million New Zealanders of the past thousand years or so, and especially the pakeha residents of the last century, have wrought tremendous changes to the island landscapes. Maori agriculture was basically conservationist, with land being left to regain its fertility after a few years of cropping. But the pakeha were exploiters. A grassland-based agriculture was imposed, involving major modifications to the native flora and fauna. Many new plant species were introduced. Mammals, too, were brought in, not only the pigs, sheep, cattle and horses necessary for farm production, but also stoats and weasels, possums, rabbits and deer. And even species of British birds, such as sparrows and thrushes, were established. Part of this large-scale reorganisation of New Zealand's fauna was intended to deal with such things as insect plagues, by predators known to the settlers. But another part was the desire to recreate the British scene. Acclimatisation societies were set up to aid the introduction and establishment processes; they still operate, mainly to provide the raw materials for hunters, shooters and fishermen. British flora were brought in, too, not only trees such as the oak and horse chestnut but bushes like gorse and blackberry, intended for hedges but soon to run wild over many hundreds of square kilometres of countryside. Indeed, so involved were the settlers in the idea of creating another Britain in the southern hemisphere that they even erected public buildings with all of their windows facing south!

The environments which the pakeha colonists invaded were finely balanced. The forest and tussock grassland covers, for example, were necessary restraints on soil erosion by natural processes. Felling and persistent burning, efforts aimed at increasing the productivity of the grasslands, opened the soil to the ravages of rain, frost, and wind; browsing animals—sheep, cattle, deer, and rabbits—hindered tree regeneration and compacted the soil, while, if there were too many in a given area, removing the grass cover, leaving bare hillsides to be severely eroded during heavy rains and strong winds. Thus soil erosion rapidly became a major problem. Large scars on hillsides mark the removal of immense volumes of materials; deep gullies trace the work of running water; rivers choked with gravel and silt indicate the amount of material which is being lost; floods have increased in frequency since forest removal accelerated rates of run-off across and through the soil. Indeed, such a proportion of the country's surface is so easily eroded that earth movements of various kinds form a major hazard to overland communications.

General public concern about such environmental problems is recent, though the need for conservation of water and soil resources has been recognised in some quarters for several decades. One-thirteenth of the country is now enclosed within National Parks, which, unlike their British counterparts, are mainly beyond the farming frontier. Commercial activity is generally prohibited in these, but there are current controversies over the possibilities of mineral exploitation. In 1941, a Soil Conservation Act was passed, and most of the country is now served by elected Catchment Boards—as well as Pest Destruction and Rabbit Boards—whose task is to protect the environment and generate wise land use. Work has been directed in particular to the river headwaters, aiming to reduce erosion, to restrict the downstream movement of soil materials by afforestation and the 'resting' of over-grazed land. Notable among the schemes, both for its size and its success, is one that concerned the Molesworth Station in the high country of inland Marlborough. This land was notorious for its ravaged state, the consequence of over-grazing and the depredations of rabbits, but several decades of careful husbanding by employees of the Department of Lands and Survey has culminated in its current commercial viability as a cattle station and its new environmental balance.

Many institutions, both public and private, have been established in recent years to act as environmental watchdogs. A major catalyst for this activity was a growing campaign, which peaked in the late 1960s, aimed at preventing any action to raise Lake Manapouri, in Fiordland National Park, to provide cheap electricity which successive governments had contracted to sell to a company constructing an aluminium smelter near to Invercargill. This was a successful campaign. It led also to the initiation of an Environmental Council, which is an advisory body to government, a Ministry for the Environment, and an independent Commissioner for the Environment who audits environmental impact reports prepared for all proposed public works. (Unfortunately, the reports are prepared by the departments advancing the proposals.) In addition, attempts are being made to control the quality of the coastal and inland waters, to protect particularly valuable sites as scenic reserves and areas of special scientific interest, and generally to correct the ravages of more than a century's exploitation of the land, replacing such attitudes by policies which will protect and preserve the environment in the face of the growing demands of an increasingly technological society.

NATIONAL CHARACTER

Most New Zealanders come from one of only two basic ethnic stocks, and there are only about three million of them. Nevertheless, to generalise about their characteristics is a far from easy task. The stereotyped New Zealander reflects the pioneer tradition: male, lean, hard-working, an outdoor type, satisfied with, and intensely proud of, his way of life, and vociferous in its defence; his womenfolk are in the background. Elements of this remain in the predominantly urban society today. Frequently, too, the New Zealander is represented as an eternal optimist, as reflected in the catch-phrase 'She'll be right'; when this optimism proves to be unfounded, there is a general tendency to expect solutions from central government.

If these, like all stereotypes, contain little more than a grain of truth, they do injustice, both to pakeha society on which they are based and to the very different Maori society. Reasonable generalisations can be made, however, about the type of society which New Zealanders—almost entirely pakeha New Zealanders—have created for themselves, and these generalisations form the basis for the remainder of the book. New Zealand society contains a deep humanitarian streak, one which is reflected in the egalitarian social policies erected to protect residents from the vicissitudes of a laissez-faire economic system. These have ensured relatively high material standards of living (on an international scale) for a larger proportion of the population than is perhaps usual; to provide these, a highly centralised, strongly bureaucratic administrative structure has been produced. And finally, despite the many caveats which a detailed critique would have to make, New Zealand has been much more successful than most countries in developing a truly multi-racial society.

2

How the Country is Run

As a member of the Commonwealth, New Zealand's head of state is the British monarch, known since 1974 as the Queen of New Zealand; she is represented locally by a governor-general, at present Sir Denis Blundell (the second New Zealander to hold the post). The governor-general has no executive power, all of which is in the hands of the Executive Council, which comprises the Cabinet advising him. The Cabinet is answerable to the House of Representatives, which has a single chamber and is elected by universal adult suffrage.

A constitution was written for New Zealand in 1852, but since then virtually all of its clauses have been either rendered obsolete or replaced; one of the country's leading political scientists has described New Zealand's lack of a written constitution as 'look, no hands' government! Initially there was a number of checks to the power of the House of Representatives, including the governor-general and the Legislative Council. The latter, in particular, could amend and defeat bills coming from the lower chamber but when the term of office of appointees was changed in 1891 from life to seven years it became much more a place of political patronage and lost its teeth; it was abolished in 1950. There was also a series of provinces, originally six, then ten, but eventually nine, which were necessary for the local government of the isolated pioneer settlements. Probably their most important function was the leasing and sale of crown land, but in 1876 the bankrupt provinces were abolished and all functions except the most parochial were assumed by the central government, which has been located at Wellington since 1865.

There are at present eighty-seven members of the House of Representatives, each representing a particular constituency. Four are members for the Maori population, their seats having been created in 1852 because, as Maoris hold their land communally, they were otherwise disenfranchised by the ruling property qualification. (There were similar seats for the goldfields' residents in the 1860s.) After the introduction of adult male suffrage in 1879, however, the Maori seats were not removed and since then there has been general apathy among both Maori and pakeha concerning the topic of separate representation. At present the Maori constituencies represent many more adult residents than do the eighty-three others and, because most Maori live in the north of the North Island, the Southern Maori constituency covers all of the South Island plus the North Island south of a Hastings–Palmerston North line (approximately). Many Maoris do not register as voters, however.

Although New Zealand is a small country, it is active in international affairs and has a considerable state involvement in most aspects of society and economy. Thus a large administrative burden falls on the eighty-seven MPs, particularly those of the government of the day. A Cabinet of about twenty members is typical of recent governments, which means that a member of the government party has perhaps a forty per cent chance of being in the Cabinet (compared with about seven per cent for a British MP). There are also about fifteen Parliamentary Select Committees, which review legislation; members of both parties, including Cabinet ministers, sit on these, and, for the average minister, there are several portfolios to be administered, as shown by the list of those held by the twenty ministers in the first year of the 1972 Labour Government.

1   Prime Minister; Minister of Foreign Affairs; Minister in Charge of Audit Dept, Legislative Dept, Security, Intelligence Service
2   Deputy Prime Minister; Minister of Labour, Works and Development; Minister in Charge of Publicity

3 Minister of Trade and Industry; Energy Resources
4 Minister of Finance; Minister in Charge of Dept of Statistics, Friendly Societies
5 Minister of Justice; Attorney-General; Minister in Charge of Civil Aviation
6 Minister of Maori Affairs, Lands
7 Minister of Police, Customs; Associate Minister of Finance
8 Minister of Defence; Minister in Charge of War Pensions, Rehabilitation
9 Minister of Social Welfare; Minister in Charge of the Government Printing Office
10 Minister of State Services, Health
11 Minister of Agriculture and Fisheries, Forests, Science
12 Minister of Housing; Minister in Charge of State Advances Corporation, Earthquake and War Damage Commission, Public Trust Office
13 Minister of Local Government, Internal Affairs; Minister in Charge of Valuation Department
14 Minister of Transport; Minister in Charge of State Insurance Office
15 Minister of Education, Island Affairs
16 Minister of Tourism; Associate Minister of Social Welfare
17 Minister of Overseas Trade, for the Environment, of Recreation and Sport; Associate Minister of Foreign Affairs
18 Minister of Immigration, Mines; Associate Minister of Works and Development
19 Minister of Railways, Electricity, Civil Defence
20 Postmaster-General; Minister of Broadcasting; Minister in Charge of Government Life Insurance Office

THE VOTING SYSTEM

Elections must be held at least triennially and few parliaments do not serve their full term (the last that did not was elected in 1949 and called for a new House in 1951). Registra-

C

tion as a voter is compulsory for all New Zealand citizens (including those from Great Britain), each of whom has one vote in the constituency where he lives. The candidate obtaining most votes in the constituency is elected as its member.

All adults over 18 have the vote; males over 21 since 1879, females over 21 since 1893 (New Zealand was third to the State of Wyoming and the Island of Pitcairn in granting female suffrage). The voting age was lowered to 20 in 1972, and 18 in 1974. Persons who are more than fifty per cent Maori in their ancestry (a qualification which is not provable) must register on the rolls for the Maori seats. Other Maoris may choose the Maori or the pakeha rolls, and there is some transfer from one to the other and back again. Electoral rolls are re-compiled for every alternate election (ie every six years, on average), and are adjusted for the intervening general election and any necessary by-elections. Voters who die are removed from the roll by the Registrar of Electors; those who reach the voting age or who move to another constituency are themselves responsible for ensuring that they are on the relevant roll.

Voting, invariably on a Saturday, is not obligatory, but the turnout is usually high (eighty-nine per cent in 1972). Individuals may vote at any polling booth, not necessarily within their home constituency, and the voting act involves crossing out the names of all the candidates the elector does not support, rather than the more usual method of placing an 'X' beside the name of the favoured candidate. Votes are counted, and published, by booth and results are known within a few hours of the end of polling, though special votes (cast away from the elector's constituency) may delay the final decision for a week or more.

The non-Maori electorates vary little in their number of voters. A rural 'quota' which made country seats twenty-eight per cent smaller than urban ones was abolished in 1945. The number of seats is now related to population growth, and the total for the South Island is fixed at twenty-five. After each quinquennial census, the Representation Commission divides the South Island population by twenty-five to find an average number per constituency, and this is used to determine the number of seats in the North Island. The Commission then draws electoral boundaries, changing them as little as possible from the previous set, with no constituency having more than five per cent either greater or less than the average number of voters. Four public servants, an independent chairman, and a nominee of each of the Government and the opposition form the Commission.

This electoral system, like the British one on which it is based, occasionally produces a different pattern of party representation in the House compared with party proportions of votes cast over the whole country. It also tends to produce a two-party house, with minority groups finding it very hard to win seats. One of its major advantages is the fairly low ratio of voters to member, which encourages high accessibility of constituents to their representatives. Most MPs hold frequent constituency 'surgeries' and perform many non-partisan functions on behalf of voters.

The triennial general elections are the major elements of public participation in political decision-making. There is a provision for referenda, but these are held infrequently. The most recent were in 1949, when the questions concerned later closing hours for public-houses (defeated), compulsory military service (accepted), and a government betting agency (accepted), and in 1967, concerning later hours again (this time accepted) and extension of the parliamentary term to four years (defeated). At every general election since 1896 there has also been a liquor referendum, at which the public choose between Prohibition, National Continuance, or State Control (see Chapter 5). This referendum was cancelled in 1931, to reduce public expenditure.

PARTIES AND POLICIES

For most of the twentieth century, political life in New Zealand has been dominated by two main parties—though the same two only since the mid-1930s. These two parties, since there are no substantial economic class differences within the country, must compete for the votes of a large 'middle class' and therefore present their policy differences in delicate hues rather than in clear colours.

The younger of the present main parties, National, was an amalgamation and reformation of two which were soundly beaten in the 1935 election. It has held power for two long periods—1949 to 1957, and 1960 to 1972—under only three prime ministers—Sir Sidney Holland to 1957, Sir Keith Holyoake from 1957 to 1972 and Sir Jack Marshall, in the final year. National's basic philosophy favours free enterprise, and much of its support is drawn from the business and farming communities. Nevertheless, it accepts the need for government regulation of economic and social affairs and has continued, often reluctantly and certainly without much innovative or expansive activity, the welfare state structure inherited from its predecessors. The present leader is Robert Muldoon; both Sir Jack Marshall and Sir Keith Holyoake were on his front bench in 1974.

The Labour Party grew as the political wing of trade unionism; it does not subscribe to socialist philosophy, however, although many of its early members and MPs were more committed to radical change of society than is the present generation. Like National, it is largely pragmatic in its choice of policies, though its basic sympathies are clearly towards worker rather than employer, towards humanitarianism rather than economic development first and foremost, towards urban rather than rural interests, towards national rather than Commonwealth needs. After long apprenticeship in opposition, Labour gained power by a landslide victory at the end of the depression in 1935, with widespread support in many small farming areas as well as in towns and cities. Between then and 1949 it wrought great changes in the welfare state, but stuck to orthodox attitudes in financial policy. A brief period of power from 1957 to 1960 was won through the offer of substantial tax concessions during the campaign, and then lost, it is often said, by the tough 'black Budget' of 1958 which, among other things, raised taxes on beer, tobacco and petrol. Control of the government benches was regained in 1972, after a campaign based on 'Time for a Change' and which pursued particular sectional and local interests. Its leader, Normal Kirk, died in 1974 and he was replaced by Bill Rowling.

These two parties draw their basic support from well-defined sectors within New Zealand society—National from business and farming, Labour from industrial and service workers, which is suggestive of class differences but no longer reflects inter-class strife. (The 'workers of the world unite' type of campaigning is long gone!) A result of such loyalties, however, is that certain places have more say than others in determining election outcomes. Rural districts are staunchly National (or at least, anti-Labour—see below on Social Credit): in the large cities, the 'better' suburbs also strongly favour National, those housing lower income groups vote for Labour, and there are a few marginals which mix the two groups. It is in the provincial centres—Napier and Gisborne, for example, or Whangarei and Rotorua—that most marginal seats are located, where the two urban 'classes', plus some farming communities, are combined in the same constituency. Most rural and large city constituencies are 'safe seats', immune to even large swings against their incumbents; the provincial centre constituencies are where several recent elections have been won and lost.

Only one minority party has consistently contested most seats at recent elections, the Social Credit Political League. Founded to propound Major Douglas's financial theories ('funny money'), this for a long time acted as a pressure group on the main parties, hoping, in particular, to influence Labour. It entered elections in 1954, winning a surprising eleven per cent of all votes, many in urban areas. It polled well in succeeding contests, reaching a peak of fourteen per cent of all votes in 1966, when it gained one seat in the House. During that time it became very much a rural protest party, with especially strong support among dairy farmers. A major problem has been whether to remain as a campaigner for monetary reform or to broaden its policy and become an alternative potential opposition. More and more it has become the latter, but its inability to win seats has been frustrating to the party and a catalyst for internal problems. Prior to the 1972 election, the party split; Social Credit then gained seven per cent of the votes and the splinter group, the New Democratic Party, less than two per cent.

The four Maori seats sat outside the main political arena until after the 1935 Labour victory, when the members—those representing the Ratana religion—affiliated with the government. Since then, the Maori constituencies have been Labour's safest seats; turnout in them is usually very low, and the majority very large. From 1946 to 1949, when Labour held a majority of four, it was often claimed that they ruled on the Maori vote.

New Zealand's politicians are probably more representative of the society at large than are those of many other countries. This reflects a general New Zealand mistrust of the expert and support for the average man—which came to the fore with the rule of R. J. Seddon ('King Dick') from 1892 to 1906—and a relatively low image of political life as a worthwhile career. Thus only two of the country's prime ministers (J. R. Marshall and W. E. Rowling) in the present century have been university graduates; two other recent leaders have had very limited formal education. Each of the present parties comprises members representing their main areas of support; National is populated largely by farmers, businessmen, and lawyers, and Labour by trade unionists and a greater number of 'professional' or 'lifetime' politicians.

Election of one of the parties to government gives it what amounts to absolute power for the next three years. The opposition party is a weak element in the system of running the country; it can scrutinise and delay legislation but cannot defeat it without defections from the government side. And there is no upper house to act as a further scrutineer. Parliament's role is thus merely to prevent gross abuses of power only, which it can do in most cases since changes in the Electoral Act—in many senses New Zealand's constitution—require the support of either three-quarters of all MPs or of a majority of valid votes at a referendum.

Rule by party can, in many matters, be concealed from the public view since decisions are made by Cabinet, passed to the parliamentary party at a private meeting (termed *Caucus*) and then, if necessary, passed through the House. (An alternative method of making legislation is through an order in Executive Council.) Such secrecy is probably greatest when Labour is in power, since this is a more tightly-knit group. Members of a Labour cabinet are elected by the Caucus and the prime minister can only allot them to portfolios; National Party prime ministers make their own appointments.

Parliament's impotence is in many areas countered by the role of pressure groups. Largest, most notable, and widest-ranging are the Federation of Labour, representing virtually all trade unions, the Public Service Association, representing most government employees, the Employers' Federation, the Manufacturers' Federation, and Federated Farmers; certain section groups—such as the brewers and the Returned Service-men's Association—make strong representation on particular issues. Drafting of important legislation is usually preceded by consultation between government and relevant groups—consultation afterwards discussed by both parties with the mass media. On many issues, the pressure groups probably exert more influence than non-Cabinet members of the government party, let alone the opposition. Indeed, ministers are probably more responsive to the general public. There is a New Zealand tradition of letters to the editors of newspapers being referred to relevant ministers or officials for public reply. Today, current affairs programmes on TV seem to be taking over this role; during one controversy in 1972 a minister stated, in a news interview, which programme he would appear on, and who should interview him, and during another, in 1971, a strike of postal workers was concluded.

LOCAL GOVERNMENT

New Zealand has had local governments since the intro-duction of responsible government; the present system dates from the dissolution of the provinces in 1876. There are two basic units, counties and municipalities; most of the latter are boroughs, though some of the larger places bear the title of city (but perform no extra functions). Counties are divided into ridings and many contain semi-autonomous town districts.

In contrast with Britain, Canada and the United States, local governments in New Zealand perform few important functions.

A major difference, for example, is the lack of any local government role in New Zealand's education ·system. Provision of roads and streets, of basic utilities such as water, electricity, sewage and rubbish disposal, and, if needed, of public transport, are the major county and borough activities, along with the preparation of planning schemes. But in many cases, even these functions have been yielded up, especially in the larger urban areas which comprise a major central city, and a patchwork of boroughs, county ridings, and town districts, most of which strongly resist any moves for amalgamation. To overcome administrative multiplicity, *ad hoc* boards have been created to provide facilities for the whole urban area, such as fire services and hospitals, harbours and drainage, public transport and electricity; some of these boards are run by elected members. There are also Regional Planning Authorities, which are advisory to local governments.

Local governments are elected triennially; all seats on all bodies are voted for, throughout the country, on the same day, although some areas now have voting spread over a week and others operate a postal ballot. Most candidates stand as independents, and political parties are active only in the main cities. Ward systems are not usual so that, for example, Christchurch electors in 1971 had to select 1 candidate from 3 for mayor, 19 from 43 for city councillor, 9 from 19 for the Drainage Board, 5 from 11 for the Harbour Board, 7 from 16 for the Hospital Board, and 6 from 13 for the Transport Board (there was no contest for the seats on the Catchment Board). All ratepayers (property-owners) are registered as voters by right; all other adults aged 18 and over are entitled to be registered, on application. In counties, but not boroughs and cities, ratepayers have had three votes, and other residents one, in each election; this was changed in 1973 to 'one person, one vote'.

Rates on property values (either the unimproved land value, the value of capital improvements, including buildings, or both) are the main source of local body revenue; property valuations are provided every five years by a central government department. There are no local sales taxes apart from a four cents levy on every gallon of petrol sold in an area, which is distributed among that area's constituent local governments (but not the *ad hoc* boards). Public loans can be raised only with central government approval, thereby ensuring that there are not too many calls on the underwriters and also providing a mechanism for regulating the economy. Government grants and loans are available for many projects; central government builds and maintains major highways, for example.

Reform of local government is a continuing issue. There have been some voluntary amalgamations recently, most involving small rural areas. But small bodies within large urban areas are usually very loath to part with their sovereignty, partly because they wish to retain their autonomy and often because they can operate with lower rates. Local government commissions have produced amalgamation schemes but these are rarely accepted locally and central governments are reluctant to impose them, because of possible electoral consequences.

THE REGULATED STATE

Central governments in New Zealand are deeply involved in regulation of the country's economy. Legislation producing this involvement has been introduced throughout the last hundred years, but in particular after two major economic depressions, the first in the 1880s and the other in the 1930s.

A main concern of early governments—the provincial bodies prior to 1876—was the development of the land resource. This crystallised in the 1880s into a debate over land tenure and farm size, a conflict between large leaseholds and small freeholds. In the 1890s, the 'small man' won, with many of the large estates being subdivided by the government and leased in perpetuity (999 years); loans at five per cent interest were advanced to the new farmers. Shorter leases and the opportunity to purchase freehold were introduced in 1907; most good agricultural land is now owned in freehold but nearly one-third of the country, most of its poorer, higher land, is still leased.

Opening-up the country away from the coast required people and a transport system; governments provided both. The original company settlements and the provincial governments used income from land sales to finance immigration; in 1874, 31,000 assisted immigrants landed in New Zealand. The provinces started the rail and road systems. The central government took them over in the 1870s and rapidly expanded their limbs; a telegraph system was also installed. Since then, sponsored immigration and public works have been major elements in the country's economic growth.

Two main themes dominate government regulation of the New Zealand economy; support for the export earners, and the weaning of local industries to reduce dependence on overseas sources. Protection of the farmers is largely provided by twenty-nine statutory authorities, some the outcome of wartime measures when governments bought all farm production at prescribed prices. Marketing is a major role for these authorities, though some are more widely influential. The Meat Board, for example, negotiates freight rates and shipping services, grades meat, promotes overseas sales, and, through a separate company, sells meat. It also, like several other boards, operates a minimum price reserve scheme, financed by a levy on all meat exported. The Apple and Pear Board buys all of the country's produce—except that sold locally in small lots—at a fixed price, and arranges the local and overseas sales. Although statutory bodies, these operations are not under direct government control; rather they are run by elected members. Government is active in many other ways, however, as in the fostering of research and the bargaining for trade agreements, notably those which preceded British entry to the EEC.

Manufacturing industries were first protected by tariffs introduced in the 1880s, although there is a longer history of customs duties. Many tariffs were removed in the early twentieth century, to be replaced in 1938 by a system of import licensing. According to this, a schedule is produced annually indicating the amounts of a clearly-defined, wide range of goods which can be imported in the coming year, and would-be importers then apply for licences. By its omissions and its quotas, this list protects local manufacturers and limits the amount of foreign exchange spent. There is continuing debate on the relative value of this system and that of a series of tariffs, not only as means of supporting local industry but also of correcting balance of payments problems and reducing local inflation.

The absence of any government committed to state socialism means that there are no nationalised industries although some utilities, the railways, the airlines and many of the coal mines, as well as the Reserve Bank and one trading bank, are state-owned. Governments have also invested in enterprises which they wished to foster, as in the pulp and paper industry, but there is growing concern about the growth of foreign ownership of New Zealand industry. (At present this amounts to only five per cent of companies, but thirty-five per cent of all plant and machinery.) During the 1960s, and culminating in the National Development Conference of 1968, the Government entered the field of 'indicative planning', setting growth targets for various sectors of the economy necessary for a given desired growth rate in the gross national product. There was also a debate about problems of regional variations in growth rates, and the growing dominance of Auckland over the country's economy, which led to the introduction in 1972 of mild measures aimed to reduce these disparities.

BANKING AND CURRENCY

Regulation of a country's economy by government requires state control over currency and credit. The major instrument of such policy in New Zealand is the Reserve Bank, established in 1934 to control the currency; it was fully nationalised in 1936, and has sole rights to issue money. It is a banker's bank, with which the five trading banks must lodge a given percentage of their deposits. The trading banks—the Bank of New Zealand (which is state-owned), the Australian and New Zealand Bank, the Bank of New South Wales, the Commercial Bank of Australia, and the National Bank of New Zealand—act as depositers and lenders, operate chequing systems and savings banks. There are also thirteen regional Trustee Savings Banks, which are similar to the Post Office Savings Bank except for their wider range of customer services including, as a 'bait' for depositers, the ability to grant housing mortgages. Increasingly, the trustee banks are competing with the established trading banks in their established functions.

Monetary policy in New Zealand aims to control both the internal financial situation—particularly, in recent years, the rate of inflation—and the balance of overseas payments (a critical function in a country so dependent on foreign trade for its prosperity). In many countries, such control is exercised by the manipulation of interest rates, but in New Zealand low interest rates are maintained (the maximum which can be offered, for any fixed term, to a depositer is fixed by statute). This policy benefits both the government as a borrower and also key industries, such as agriculture and housing. Thus the amount of money circulating is controlled by varying the proportion of a financial institution's deposits which must be held in Government securities, at fixed rates. Credit is varied in its volume, but not its cost, therefore; outstanding overdrafts in 1971 were at an average interest rate of only 6·1 per cent.

New Zealand's currency, the $NZ, was introduced in 1967 to replace the pound (£NZ): each pound became two dollars, a dollar being divided into a hundred cents. Notes are issued for one, two, five, ten and twenty dollars; copper currency is for one and two cents, and cupro-nickel currency for five, ten, twenty and fifty cents. The change in the currency followed about a year after a similar change in Australia, and represented part of a continuing trend of independence from Britain. Before 1933, only UK silver coinage circulated in New Zealand; in that year, a new exchange rate of £125NZ to £100UK was introduced. There was devaluation in 1967 and, since the decision to 'float' the British pound in 1972, New Zealand's currency has strengthened, aided by a revaluation in 1973, but there were devaluations in 1974 and 1975.

THE WELFARE STATE

To many foreigners, New Zealand is best known for its green grass, its butter and lamb, and its 'All Blacks'; to many others it is renowned for its welfare state. This has a long history, reflecting a deep humanitarian streak in New Zealanders, although many of its provisions were erected to counter the individual problems created by economic depression.

One fundamental of the welfare state policy concerns the maintenance of full employment, and of good working conditions, plus the receipt of adequate wages. The first industrial legislation followed the depression and strikes of the late 1880s, being introduced by the socialist—Pember Reeves—who was a member of the first two Liberal governments. Most significant was the Industrial Conciliation and Arbitration Act of 1894 which was intended both to stimulate and protect trade unions. The basic form of this act has provided a continuing basis for industrial relations in New Zealand (see Chapter 4).

The other fundamental element of the welfare state is the social security system. Old-age pensions were introduced in 1898, pensions for women and children in 1911, family benefits (allowances) in 1926, and invalid benefits in 1936. The Social Security Act of 1938 articulated this structure and introduced more provisions, such as universal superannuation and a comprehensive medical system. A full public education system has been devised, cheap loans for housing provided, and a number of other bodies—such as the Public Trustee, the Earthquake and War Damage Commission and the State Insurance Office (established in the 1860s)—provide a wide range of services. (For fuller details, see Chapter 3.)

THE PUBLIC SERVICE

Running a regulated and welfare state such as New Zealand requires a large bureaucracy. Indeed, with one-fifth of all the country's workers—including the postal and railway workers, plus the school teachers—in its service, the government is by far the largest employer. And since virtually all of the legislation is operated by central rather than by local government, most of these state employees are in the one public service. The New Zealand Public Service Association, the trade union for many government employees, is the largest in the country, with more than 49,000 members.

The public service, with its thirty-seven departments, is a

career service, with little outside competition for 'élite' posts. There is an increasing graduate entry, however, especially into departments such as Foreign Affairs and the scientific and research organisations. Running of the service is controlled (to avoid political patronage) by a four-member State Services Commission, which grades all posts and servants. Posts are advertised and appointments are open to appeal: in 1971 the then vice-chancellor of the University of Otago was appointed to be director of education, but he lost the job on appeal, to an administrator who had risen through the career service.

TAXATION

Running New Zealand's regulated and welfare state also requires money, of which direct taxes provide two-thirds. Indirect taxes—notably sales and customs duties (forty per cent on imported cars)—provide a further quarter of the revenue. Other income comes from profits on the operation of government enterprises, notably the Post Office, and from occasional overseas loans.

Income tax is deducted from all employees on a Pay-as-you-Earn basis, each person being coded at the beginning of the tax year (May 1) according to marital status. At the end of the year, a tax return is filed on which details of income received and tax paid (supplied by the employer) are entered and exemptions are claimed. The most important exemptions are: for the taxpayer and a dependent spouse; for life, accident and sickness insurance premiums (including superannuation) up to a certain level; and for charitable donations. There is no claim for dependent children on whom the family benefit is claimed. The tax due is then computed, and the taxpayer may be owed a refund.

For three decades there was a separate social security tax (of 1s 6d [7½p] in the £1 when it was abolished) which was paid as a flat rate by all taxpayers. Now, however, there is a single sliding scale. Tax rates appear at first glance to be high, but it must be remembered that there is relatively little indirect taxation, that there is an extensive welfare state to be supported, and that local government rates are low as most services are centrally financed. (The average urban property owner pays perhaps a little over $100 annually in rates to a local authority.) If we take a married man, with a non-working wife, who invests 10 per cent of his income in insurance, his tax at various incomes in 1974 would be:

Total Income $	Taxable Income $	Tax Paid $	Tax as % of Income
2,000	1,250	159.31	7·9
4,000	3,030	586.81	14·6
6,000	4,850	1,195.66	19·6
8,000	6,650	1,915.51	23·9
10,000	8,450	2,679.41	26·8
12,000	10,250	3,458.26	25·8

For every taxable dollar above 12,000 that is earned, the tax was a flat rate of 45 cents, which leads to the charge that New Zealand's tax structure hits hardest at the middle-income earners. Only 80,000 New Zealanders earned more than $10,000 in 1972–3, however.

THE LEGAL SYSTEM

The legal system in New Zealand is based on British common law and, in the absence of any New Zealand law or precedent, British precedents prevail. As befits a small country, the legal system is a simple one. There are three courts. At the lowest level are the Magistrates' Courts, operated by salaried, stipendiary magistrates. Cases are dealt with speedily and relatively cheaply. Justices of the Peace may hear cases in these courts, but their main function is in the administration of oaths. The next level comprises the Supreme Court, which functions as do the separate courts and divisions in Great Britain. It tries certain cases and also hears appeals against decisions of the Magistrates' Courts. Finally, there is the Court of Appeal, although certain cases may be given leave to proceed to the Privy Council. There are also special courts for particular functions, such as those for Land Valuation, Arbitration, and Maori Land. Jury service is applied to all persons aged between 21 and 65, other than public servants.

Daily administration of the law is in the hands of a centrally-organised police service, members of which are unarmed. In 1972, there were 3,302 policemen, one to every 880 residents. There is also a separate traffic police force, most of whose officers are under the control of the Ministry of Transport; some are employees of local governments. Besides policing the country's roads, these officers also conduct driving tests. Crime rates are not high; on average, one adult in sixty is involved in a non-traffic offence each year, one in twelve in a traffic offence. The prisons hold about 2,600 inmates, only 130 of them females.

Protection of citizens' rights in dealing with central government departments is provided by an Ombudsman, first appointed in 1962, who acts either on specific complaints or on his own initiative. He has no statutory rights to impose solutions, and his powers do not extend to local government activities.

DEFENCE

New Zealand's armed forces, particularly its army, have a long and honourable tradition of service in time of war. This began with the Boer War, when 6,500 men served, of whom 228

Mts Cook (right) and Tasman reflected in the waters of Lake Matheson, Westland.

died. During the 1914–18 war, 124,000 New Zealanders
(91,000 of them volunteers) saw service; this was ten per cent of
the country's total population, or forty per cent of all males aged
between 20 and 45. Of these, 16,000 died, and another 42,000
were injured. World War II saw 194,000 serve (sixty-seven per
cent of males aged 18–45), of whom 12,000 died. Since then,
New Zealand troops have been active in Korea, Malaysia and
Vietnam. A major controversy has developed in nearly every
one of these wars over the question of conscription; it was particularly fierce during 1914–18 when many persons of Irish
descent feared they would be sent to fight in Eire. At present,
there is a regular force plus a ballotted (by birthdates) territorial force, whose members must attend twenty days of training
(including fourteen days in a camp) in each of three consecutive
years.

The present defence forces comprise 12,500 men, 5,500 in the
Army, 4,000 in the Air Force, and 3,000 in the Navy. Apart
from the base at Singapore, all of these are stationed in New
Zealand. Total expenditure on defence is only two per cent of
the gross national product—six per cent of all government
expenditure.

Returned servicemen have always been favourably treated in

New Zealand's sprawling urban giant, Auckland (population
650,000) looking south over the Waitemata Harbour. Much of
the suburban North Shore shown in the foreground was developed after the opening of the Harbour Bridge in 1959, and is
typical of the low density, bungalow landscape which characterises New Zealand's towns and cities. High-rise development
is nearly all concentrated into the one steep-sided, narrow
valley which houses the city centre.

The nation's capital, Wellington, with the many office blocks
erected during recent years. Some two-storey weatherboard
homes, typical of the nineteenth century, can be seen in the
foreground. Parliament Buildings are in the right centre, facing
the large, weatherboard block of government offices. The city
centre is hemmed in between the shoreline and the steep front
cliff of The Terrace, which is reached by cablecar.

New Zealand, as have the dependants of those who were killed in action and those who returned home disabled. Apart from pensions, money to provide assistance in housing, furniture purchase, trade training and education, for example, has been widely available. Loans have also been offered, at special rates, to allow ex-servicemen to set themselves up as farmers, and soldier settlement schemes are characteristic of several areas.

EXTERNAL AFFAIRS

As already stressed, New Zealand for long followed Britain's lead in foreign affairs and it was only in the 1930's that an independent policy was really initiated. Thus most of its links have been associated with Britain and the other major Commonwealth nations; others have been developed where they are beneficial to New Zealand's present and potential overseas trade. In recent years, there has been growing interest in, and association with, the countries of Southeast Asia, and links with South America are being forged. New Zealand's overseas representation, and the reciprocal overseas representation in Wellington, is therefore with Britain and the former Commonwealth Dominions, with the other 'Great Powers' (including China), and with countries of Western Europe, Southeast Asia, the Pacific and South America.

Within the South Pacific, New Zealand is responsible for several small countries. It administers the Ross Dependency in Antarctica, plus several sub-Antarctic islands (Christchurch is the base for American Antarctic operations); the Tokelau Islands are a legal part of New Zealand; Niue has internal self-government but its external affairs are handled by New Zealand; the Cook Islands are self-governing in free association with New Zealand. Citizens of all of these places have free right of entry, as residents, to New Zealand, as did Western Samoans until they became independent of New Zealand's League of Nations/United Nations trusteeship in 1962.

New Zealand has never aimed for an important role in world affairs, though it played a significant part in the establishment of the United Nations, especially its non-political associations.

Recently, it has become active in schemes for regional co-operation and development in the South Pacific and Asia. Over half of the country's overseas aid goes to the former area, particularly Fiji, Niue, Western Samoa, and the Cook Islands; over forty per cent goes to Asia, notably Bangladesh, Indonesia and Malaysia in recent years. New Zealand's present Labour government seeks moral leadership in the South Pacific, a role which gained world prominence in its actions against the 1973 and 1974 French nuclear tests at Mururoa Atoll.

POSTSCRIPT

The general election of 29 November 1975 saw National returned to power, with a landslide victory similar to that which brought in Labour three years earlier. The campaign was built on the twin pillars of the relative merits of the two new leaders—the relatively quiet Bill Rowling and the ebullient Robert Muldoon—and the Labour government's performance in a period of record inflation (around 15 per cent per annum). To maintain full employment, the government had borrowed abroad very heavily, at a time when the real value of export income was falling, and it was severely attacked for this. The result suggests an emerging pattern in New Zealand since World War II, of long, relatively quiet periods of National Party rule, interspersed with brief periods of Labour power, in which much new legislation is forged.

3

How They Live

New Zealand is a suburban nation. The majority of its residents live in towns, most of them in single-family homes, set in their own grounds (the New Zealand term is 'section'). There are several reasons for the predominance of this life style. Firstly, the majority of New Zealanders are from Britain where, with the exception of parts of Scotland, tenement and apartment living has been far from common; they maintain the view that 'the Englishman's home is his castle'. Second, the original settlements were laid out when land was plentiful, and each household was given a sizeable section on which to grow food. Finally, until recent decades, most New Zealand towns and cities have been small places and high density development allowing easy access to workplaces has been unnecessary; in addition, there are high car ownership levels. Thus has developed the 'cult of the quarter-acre section' as the basis for life in New Zealand.

HOUSING

New Zealanders are well housed, in substantial dwellings which are well provided with facilities and amenities. Of the 800,000 households, one in seven live in flats; one-quarter rent their home, a further quarter own their dwelling outright, and about two-fifths are servicing a mortgage. Only about 400 do not have a water supply, about 60,000 rely on rainwater tanks, and the rest have a piped supply. Less than 4,000 have no hot water system and only 25,000 lack a flush toilet within the home; less than three per cent have no fridge; ten per cent no washing-machine; fifteen per cent no TV; and fifteen per cent no telephone; nearly half have a deep freeze.

54

Home ownership has become widely available over the last forty years, during which the proportion of renters has halved. This change has been the result of government policies, through the agency of the State Advances Corporation, which both rents homes and lends money for their purchase. Most of its activity dates from legislation introduced by the first Labour government in 1937.

State rental housing was the Corporation's main interest in the 1940s and a peak of over 4,000 homes constructed per year was attained then. In all, some 72,000 homes have been built for lower income households. During the years that National was in power after 1949, construction rates slackened markedly and about 25,000 of the homes were sold to their tenants. Since 1972, there has been a rapid upsurge in building, with the Ministry of Works and Development contracting outside firms to design and build dwellings within a cost constraint.

Most State homes are two- or three-bedroomed dwellings, many of them free-standing in their own sections, though there are both row and semi-detached units and some low-rise flats. The general standard of construction and accommodation is high. On the early estates, it was a general design principle that no two adjacent homes looked the same—variations in the orientation of a basic ground plan on the site often achieved this aim. As they matured, many of these estates became very attractive suburban areas, especially where homes were later sold to their occupiers and upkeep was good. The growing pressure for housing, however, resulted in the construction of large estates on the urban peripheries, particularly of Auckland and Wellington. These estates have been frequently criticised, both for their visual monotony and for their lack of community facilities. As a reaction to this, a wider variety of designs and of building materials is now being used, and in all blocks of land now developed, only a small proportion is occupied by State homes, thus creating a greater social and visual mixture. In general, State rental homes are provided for lower income persons, although this is not always a definite policy and some units in most towns are used to house State servants on transfer. The average cost of a State home in 1973–4 was $15,230 (plus $5,450 for land) compared with $24,000 for homes built in the private sector.

Although the designs are characteristically New Zealand, the general State housing policy regarding rental homes is not very different from that in several other countries. The State Advances Corporation is unique, however, in its other role as a cheap money-lender, thereby creating a property-owning suburban society of much wider income levels than is true in, say, Britain or North America. The basic loan is for the purchase of a new home, and is offered at five and a half per cent interest over a period of 25–30 years. Some loans are available for the purchase of older homes, though few are granted at times of a general shortage of loan money. There is a maximum loan limit, which encourages the use of the system for relatively low-cost homes, though in times of land value inflation and increasing construction costs, people are often forced to seek second and even third mortgages in the private loan market. The 1957–60 Labour government altered the scheme by making the interest rate three per cent for people whose basic income was below a certain (variable) level, and they also provided for parents to obtain, in advance, the fourteen years' family benefit payment, up to a maximum of $2,000, to use as a deposit on a home. (This is known as 'capitalising the family benefit'.) Similarly loans and capitalisation are available for needed extensions to homes. In total, the SAC provides the means for home ownership for a large group in the population which would probably otherwise not be able to buy. In 1971–2 alone, nearly 12,000 loans, totalling $46 million, were granted. Over the last decade, over 80,000 loans have been obtained, and 50,000 households have capitalised their family benefit.

Government agencies provide about one-fifth of all housing mortgage finance at the present time. The major source, according to official statistics, is 'private individuals', which includes loans made by solicitors and others acting as trustees. Savings banks provide about seven per cent of the loans, building societies and life insurance companies about ten per cent each. There are two types of building society. The permanent societies, which attract deposits and lend money to depositors, are regionally organised and are much stronger in some parts of the country, Southland for example, than they are in others, such as Wellington and Northland. The terminating building societies

—whose activities perhaps reflect the New Zealanders' love of gambling for they are illegal in Great Britain—also lend to depositors, but their attraction is the possibility of winning a ballot for an interest-free loan, which can be immediately cashed in. The latter type lend about three-quarters of all housing finance provided by building societies.

In line with general government policy on money-lending, interest rates on loans for housing are relatively low, though they are increasing and repayments are not, in contrast to Britain, tax-deductable. The average interest rate on new loans is now close to eight per cent, an increase of two percentage points in the last decade. Loans are usually for at least twenty years. Two types of mortgages are available. The table mortgage—used by government agencies and insurance companies—involves both repayment of principal and payment of interest: the flat mortgage—popular with 'solicitors' money'—involves payment of interest only; it is usually granted for a short period only—perhaps five years—with the chance of negotiation of interest rates for a further term. Just under forty per cent of mortgages are flat mortgages.

The majority of the homes occupied by New Zealand's property-owning suburbanites are single-storied. Two storeys were frequent, if not common, in the early decades of pakeha settlement—especially among the higher income groups—but the cottage or bungalow has always predominated. Some two-storey homes are built now, and there are numerous 'split-levels'. For many decades, construction was in wood, horizontal weatherboards fixed to a wooden structure, with plasterboard as an inner lining and separating rooms; the whole was topped by corrugated iron. Brick, artificial stone, and concrete blocks are now more common, especially in the South Island where timber is less easily obtained, though the first two materials (termed 'permanent materials' locally) are generally only one layer thick, being built around a wooden structure—considered desirable for protection from collapse during mild earthquakes. Tiles are now a more common roofing material, but seventy per cent of New Zealand's homes are roofed with corrugated iron; sixty per cent have weatherboard walls. Building regulations are strict, because of the earthquake hazard. Local authorities often have additional regulations with some, for example, demanding the insertion of insulating materials both in walls and ceilings. Inside, four to six rooms, plus kitchen and bathroom are common; the average floor area of new houses today is about 1,400 square feet. Showers are almost universal as are separate laundries; toilets and bathrooms are usually separate.

The house construction industry is characterised by a plethora of small firms and sub-contractors. Builders operate generally at the level of the individual home rather than on a block of several, so that they, or their customer, buy a section from a subdivider and build on it. The result is considerable local diversity within the general bungalow theme. Each city has one or more large property-developer firm which builds estates, often speculatively. Again, however, they will have several designs which are mixed together, avoiding complete homogeneity. In the past, the relatively large size of sections has allowed flexibility in the location of the dwelling. Recently, however, the rapid inflation in land values (over forty per cent in a single year), and perhaps changing attitudes to gardening also, have resulted in a reduction in the size of newly subdivided sections to around 24–28 perches (the measure of area still used for housing purposes).

The relatively small size of cities, and the property-owning, outdoor life ethos have meant little demand until recently for flats and apartments, and those needing such accommodation, like university students, have generally obtained it in subdivided older homes. There is now a strong trend away from the detached home, and over half of all new building in cities is of flats. The rising price of new homes is a factor producing this trend, but as important has been a change in the family structure. As in comparable countries, age at marriage is now very early in the twenties and child-bearing is, on average, complete by the time the parents are thirty. Many couples of fifty find their children have all left home, and they have no need for a large house and garden for the next twenty years of their married life. A smaller home is often bought, therefore; in 1965, only 545 blocks of flats were built; in 1972, 3,212.

Flat-living rarely means high-rise-living for New Zealanders, and indeed the term flat is something of a misnomer. There are some tall blocks in the largest cities, in the choicest locations and with the best views. But single-storey flats are by far the most common; the average block built in 1972 contained but three units. Typically, a block comprises two or four attached dwellings erected on a single residential section. Usually these are less spacious internally than a detached home, but the main difference is in the amount of external space. Some are built to replace obsolete older homes, thereby increasing the housing density; many are being built on newly-subdivided land throughout suburbia. In most cities, two dwellings can be put on any section, more on those in areas zoned for higher density use. This often creates design problems, since sections are developed individually, creating a cluttered appearance. Some comprehensive developments are taking place, especially of town houses in inner city areas, and zoning regulations are being relaxed to allow those. A large proportion of the 'flats' are owned by older couples and by widows, a trend which is likely to continue now that a problem over titles has been resolved and money can be borrowed on the security of the land. Those being rented are generally of slightly lower quality, at least of design, and are occupied by young couples saving to buy their own home.

Housing is not cheap in New Zealand today, though there are considerable variations both between and within cities. Thus in mid-1973, the average price paid for all houses sold in each of the four main urban areas was: Auckland, $17,513; Wellington, $18,967; Christchurch $14,964; Dunedin, $11,529. On average, over all towns, the North Island homes were $3,000 dearer than those in the South Island. For residential sections the average prices were: Auckland, $5,122; Wellington, $5,302; Christchurch, $5,512; Dunedin, $2,487. The South Island prices were about $300 cheaper, on average. Since that time there has been considerable inflation in property values, probably as much as forty per cent in the following year.

TOWNSCAPES

New Zealand towns and cities are pleasant places. Their suburbs are attractive, because the climate is favourable to grass, tree and shrub growth and there is almost universal pride in the appearance of gardens. But in general they lack character, especially on flat and undulating country where horizons are low, little real variety is visible, and the appearance of the low houses is overshadowed by street lamps and festoons of telegraph and electricity wires. (These wires are underground in new subdivisions.) Local variety is introduced by streams in some areas and there is generally ample provision of parks and play-space. In all new subdivisions, a proportion of the land must be donated to the local government as a public reserve, though the government can, and often does, opt to receive money instead if it feels that the local area is adequately provided with open space.

Fortunately most New Zealand towns and cities contain at least some hilly areas; the nation's capital is dominated by hills. These provide some local character when they are developed for housing, especially as they mature and trees grow. A variety of house designs is necessary to fit the contours, and views change constantly. In most cases, the hill suburbs are relatively expensive to build on and are occupied by higher-income groups, but they at least provide an interesting backdrop to many otherwise uninteresting townscapes. Most towns and cities have a seafront to provide some interest and focus, too; in Auckland's eastern suburbs, for example, a view of the Waitemata Harbour and its islands adds thousands of dollars to the value of many properties.

Inner suburban areas have little character, although where the weatherboard homes are gaily painted, they are far from drab. Many of these dwellings are near to the end of their lives, however, and the need for urban renewal is becoming pressing. Local governments are active in this, as are some private developers, but the problems of land assembly are severe, as most governments are reluctant to use the compulsory powers available to them. Few of the completed redevelopment schemes are particularly attractive. Local governments also build pensioner housing developments, usually clusters of short rows of one-bedroom units. Most of these are successful, but government grants often do not keep pace with rising construction costs and lower quality homes result.

Town centres have little more character than the residential areas. Some have a clear focus, like Dunedin's Octagon and Christchurch's Cathedral Square, but the short period of town-building means that none has more than a few isolated buildings of historical interest and architectural merit. Christchurch's old Supreme Court and Provincial Chambers and its new Town Hall are worth visiting for example, and there is a small number of such buildings in each city, but the town centre as a whole has no visual attraction which makes it a 'must' for the tourist. Shops are mostly one or two storeys, with much of their frontage obscured by verandahs; many are still of weatherboard, dotted among the newer concrete replacements. Tower blocks of offices and hotels are becoming more apparent, especially in Auckland and Wellington, whose cityscapes are now distinguishable from say, Sydney's or Melbourne's, only by the generally lower building profile. In the smaller towns, the commercial centre is usually one street of verandahed shops, dominated by the two-storeyed weatherboard pubs and the solidity of the post office and banks, and perhaps by the railway line on one side.

DIET

In a farming country, it is not surprising that New Zealanders eat well, and do not have to pay too much for their food (on average about thirty per cent of their incomes). Consumption of dairy products and of meat is, per head of population, about the highest in the world, although there are some interesting anomalies. Each New Zealander, on average, gets through forty pounds of butter, 250 pints of milk, 26 dozen eggs, 5 pints of cream and 33 pints of ice cream a year, but only nine pounds of cheese (which is half of the rate for the average Dane or Swede). He or she also averages about 3,000 grammes of meat per day, a similar amount to Australians and North Americans, but half as much again as British people. Surprisingly, it is beef which looms largest in this consumption, not sheepmeat, though this position is changing and may soon be reversed. Little pork, veal and offal is eaten; consumption of poultry has tripled since 1945.

As part of a stabilisation policy during World War II, several commodity prices were subsidised. A recession caused by falling wool prices led to removal of the subsidies on bread, butter and flour in 1967. Milk is still subsidised, at a cost of about forty cents per gallon, which holds the price to four cents per pint, and there is a subsidy of 3½ cents per dozen on eggs, for which the current price is about sixty cents. In mid-1974 the approximate prices for best steak were $1.30 per pound, and leg of lamb 65c per pound; butter cost 35c per pound and bread 15c for a 28oz loaf.

A good basic diet of meat and dairy products, considered monotonous by some observers, is typical in New Zealand, therefore. It is bolstered by considerable intakes of fresh fruits and vegetables, particularly of potatoes in the latter category. A quarter of all households grow some of their potatoes in their own garden, and nearly half produce some of their vegetable requirements. Canned and frozen vegetables are probably bought less frequently than in other countries but families deep freeze their own vegetable supplies (meat can be bought in bulk for deep freezing also). Many households also grow a considerable amount of fruit. Apples and soft fruits are cultivated throughout the country, whereas in the North Island, and favoured spots in some parts of the South Island, citrus fruit and grapes are also common in gardens. Much fruit—both home-grown and bought from the orchard—is bottled at home, allowing families to circumvent the seasonal shortages which are usual in the shops. ('Bottling' is a strong tradition in New Zealand, probably as a relic of the pioneer days; it was commended by a cabinet minister when there were widespread complaints against the rising cost of living in the late 1960s.)

Tea and coffee are the dominant non-alcoholic beverages. They are consumed in almost equal volume, which represents a major shift in taste since at the beginning of World War II the ratio of tea to coffee drunk was about twenty to one. Among alcoholic beverages, beer is by far the main item. The average New Zealander consumed about twenty-six gallons during 1972 —more than twice his consumption in 1938—which puts him very high among the world's beer drinkers. (If one assumes that half of the population drink virtually no beer, this means that the rest drink a pint a day.) Consumption of wine has increased six-fold in recent years, but is still only 1·2 gallons annually per person; 0·4 gallons is the average yearly intake of spirits.

Parts of the New Zealand diet are cheap, in world terms. Many other items are not, however, so that the average cost of feeding a family is not so different in New Zealand from that in comparable 'Western' countries. Many households, however, deviate from the average situation by the system of self-help, aided by the deep freeze, whereas others, such as farmworkers, get free or cheap food as part of their payment. For them, as for most of their fellow-countrymen, the basic diet is fairly cheap, if somewhat stereotyped in composition, and it is the 'extras' which are highly priced.

CONSUMER GOODS AND SHOPPING

Apart from food and shelter, clothing is the major item of expenditure for New Zealanders. In this, as with many consumer goods, the choice is between relatively expensive (by UK/US standards) locally-produced items, which are often not of high quality and offer but a small selection, or even more expensive imported goods, which may be unavailable for long periods. New Zealanders are generally well dressed, though many of them conservatively so; because of the mild and pleasant climate, there is much informality of dress, shorts, for example, being extremely common attire among males during summer. Today, major world fashion trends do not take long to reach the cities and there has been something of a clothing revolution, particularly among younger age groups (though many young people, such as university students, are much more casual in their dress than their northern hemisphere counterparts).

The variability in supplies of imported consumer goods reflects on both the strict import quotas and the vicissitudes of shipping services. Thus advertisements in newspapers announcing the arrival of a certain line in given shops are not uncommon; nor is a limit on the number of sales per shopper. A usual customer reaction is to buy as much as possible when goods are in stock rather than wait till they are needed, only to find that none are available. The alternative is the local product in which, because the market is small and producing firms few, selection is usually limited. (The major monopoly in New Zealand is in canned and frozen foods, in which one local company controls virtually the whole market: it is one of the few 'Western' countries where

Heinz beans are not available!) Many locally manufactured goods are in short supply in many parts of the country. A consequence of the present trend of population and industrial centralisation in Auckland and its surrounds is that many parts of the country find it difficult to maintain supplies from there because of transport hold-ups; the same is true of imported goods, more and more of which are entering the country through the port of Auckland. And a strike at the country's only factory producing a certain line, or, worse still, its closure, can have long-term effects so that cricket boots and golf-balls, washing powder and kitchen foil, toilet rolls and sugar may all be absent from shop shelves for weeks on end.

Some living costs, such as housing, vary considerably from place to place; others are relatively standard throughout the country. Government policy on prices is partly responsible for the standardisation; after years in which there was a differential in petrol prices according to costs of moving it from the ports, a single charge is now imposed, with no price cutting or competition by other means (such as 'free' gifts or stamps). There is a general absence of intense competition among retailers—although 'sales' seem to be ubiquitous—except in food-selling, which has seen the introduction of various price-cutting mechanisms in recent years, such as 'specials' and 'discount warehouses'. Much of this occurs only in the largest cities, and especially in Auckland, but there is little evidence in the consumer price index figures of major variations between places in costs of consumer goods.

Retailing in New Zealand is closely controlled in many ways. Apart from a few exemptions, shops operate a five-day week, opening from 9 am to 5.30 pm on four days and till 9 pm on the other (usually Friday but increasingly Thursday, thereby extending the long weekend). The exceptions are certain shopping centres, usually one in each of the large cities, which close on Monday but open all day Saturday, and the widespread corner 'dairies' which sell a wide range of goods, until well into the evening in many cases, on seven days a week (by law, certain food lines must not be sold outside 'normal' shop hours, but this is rarely enforced). In Auckland, because of its size, and Wellington, because of its extent and subdivision by hills and harbour, large suburban centres are competing with the central shopping area. The more compact Christchurch has less of this, except for food retailers in which the suburban supermarket now dominates as elsewhere, and in all other towns and cities the central shopping district still predominates; many come alive on Friday night with the traditional family expedition to 'town'.

There are about 30,000 shops in New Zealand—one to every hundred persons. On average they are small, with fewer than five working there, and a turnover of $15,000 per employed person; over half of them sell food and drink. Chain stores are slowly coming to dominate retailing and now account for about forty per cent of the sales volume; almost half of all foodstuffs sales are in self-service establishments. There is, however, still a large number of very small stores. Nearly a quarter of the country's shops have an annual turnover of less than $20,000 and only one-tenth have sales exceeding $100,000 each year. Shopping by credit is not as common as overseas; there are no local credit cards, though cheques are generally accepted, and the average New Zealander's hire purchase debt is only $40, one-sixth of that for United States' residents. Control of the amount of hire purchase credit allowed is a small element of government policies aimed to handle inflation. Minimum deposits and maximum repayment periods are set. At present these are generally ten per cent and thirty months respectively, though for cars they are fifty per cent and twenty-four months.

SOCIAL SECURITY

According to some critics of their country's welfare state, New Zealanders are 'cossetted from the cradle to the grave', a situation that breeds dependence on the State and inhibits any development of individual initiative and aspiration, which would be necessary if people had to provide for themselves in times of hardship and retirement. To other commentators, the welfare state is a marvellous example of humanitarianism at work. And to most New Zealanders, its operations are probably accepted with little question, as part now of their birthright and as evidence of the government providing for its supporters.

Apart from the possible negative, and also positive, influences of the welfare state on individual attitudes, there is no doubt that New Zealand governments, most especially those of the Labour Party, have produced a system which protects the vast majority of the population against any possible extreme financial deprivation and ensures that they are generally healthy. Access to the benefits of this system is a right of all citizens—immigrants from Australia and the United Kingdom are immediately eligible through reciprocity arrangements, but those from other countries must fulfil a residential requirement. The basic payments—family and medical benefits and superannuation—are at a flat rate and are not subject to a means test. Government revenue is used to finance the many benefits which means, because the main source of State money is the progressive income tax, that the welfare state is also a method of income redistribution. Underlying the philosophy of the system is a strong belief in the role of the family as a major social unit.

Although no longer the main item of expenditure, the family benefit is probably the one which has been paid to, or for, most New Zealanders, and is, of course, the first set of payments on the progress from cradle to grave. About one million payments, of $3 per child, are made every week; payment is for every child

------

Labour productivity is high on New Zealand farms because of the use of much machinery. Here, one farmer at Matamata in the Waikato is seen operating the herring-bone cowshed, in which he can milk several dozen cows single-handed within an hour. Note the radio, to play soothing music.

Intensive farming in the valley of the Tukituki River, just outside Waipukurau in southern Hawke's Bay. This area is a major centre of orcharding and vegetable cultivation, with freezing works and canneries at Hastings. The braided river channel is typical of the east coast of both islands.

under 16, including adopted and stepchildren, and also for those aged 16–18 who are not in employment. A cash payment can be obtained from the post office, or the benefit may be credited monthly to a Post Office Savings Bank account, in the mother's name. Since 1972, there has been no tax deduction for dependent children on whom the family benefit is received.

Care of children is provided for in a wide range of situations by the Child Welfare division of the Department of Social Welfare (the first Labour government had a separate Minister for Women and Children), and the State resumes its responsibilities for its citizens when they retire from employment or, in the case of women particularly, reach a certain age. Payments to older persons (locally termed senior citizens) are the largest items of social welfare expenditure. There are two forms of benefit, which are alternatives and not complementary. The first is the age benefit, payable to all over sixty who are retired, and to many women over fifty-five; the pension (at present about $1,000 annually) is tax-free, and income up to $676 can be earned in addition, but beyond that sum there is a reduction in benefit until at a certain level (at present $1,785 for a single and $2,686 for a married person) the payment ceases. As an alternative, the beneficiary may opt to receive the universal superannuation.

————

Another major technical innovation which has advanced the productivity of New Zealand farming is aerial topdressing, as being performed here over recently-cleared land on the eastern flanks of Mt Ruapehu, the North Island's highest peak and an active volcano.

(He or she can change from one benefit to the other as circumstances deem it desirable.) All persons over 65 with a residence qualification (twenty years in most cases) qualify for the benefit, which is the same value as the age benefit but it, and any extra income, is taxed. (For persons receiving only the benefit, of course, the tax is minimal.)

In times of rapid inflation, persons on fixed incomes such as the age benefit and universal superannuation are hard hit. Thus many people have private insurance policies to provide for their retirement, or are members of employer-sponsored superannuation schemes, the largest of which is the government scheme for State servants. Payments of premiums are tax deductible. The government introduced a comprehensive superannuation scheme based on actuarial principles in 1973 which, if it becomes effective, will provide substantial retirement benefits for future generations, as well as making the trustees of the fund the largest investors in the country.

Other social welfare payments are designed to protect incomes at times of unanticipated stress. The largest single category comprises payments to widows (those with dependent children receive more). Wives deserted by their husbands are also eligible under this scheme, as are those whose husbands have been in a mental institution for more than six months. In all cases, payment is subject to a means test. Sickness and invalid benefits are available for those temporarily prevented from working for more than eight days, and a comprehensive accident compensation scheme was introduced in 1974. Persons congenitally or accidentally incapacitated on a permanent basis, including those who are blind, are entitled to invalid benefits, and there is a special provision for incapacitated miners.

Emergency benefits and supplementary assistance can be paid in particular cases. It is perhaps a mark of the system's general success, however, that only about 25,000 such payments have been made annually in recent years, at a cost of $13 million out of the total expenditure of $33 million on social welfare benefits during 1971–2.

The citing of the value of monetary benefits conveys only a certain amount of information about social welfare schemes. More important than the actual value of a benefit is its size relative to average incomes and its rate of increase relative to general living costs. New Zealand's standard benefits for single persons are at present about thirty per cent of the average Court of Arbitration award, whereas for the married person they are just over half. As percentages of average wages earned, the benefits are slightly smaller. Since the war, these percentages have remained relatively stable, as benefits are altered to match changes in the cost of living.

MEDICAL SERVICES

The life expectancies of 75 for women and 69 for men suggest that New Zealanders are a healthy people. Indeed, they have one of the lowest infant mortality rates in the world; life expectancy at birth is greater than in Australia, Scotland, and the United States, and only slightly less than it is for Danes, English and Welsh, Norwegians, Swedes and Russians. Heart diseases are the main cause of death, followed by cancer.

Provision of health services is not entirely by the State, though there is a wide government involvement in the medical field. Public hospitals, both general and psychiatric, are run by locally-elected hospital boards, which receive central government finance. Their operations are supplemented by private hospitals, which provide one-sixth of all beds in the country. All private hospitals are registered by the Department of Health. In total, there are 199 hospitals, ranging from large city teaching establishments to small country maternity units; between them they provide approximately five beds for every 1,000 members of the population. The 'grass roots' of the medical system are the 1,300 doctors in general practice, who are supplemented by a further 1,000 employed in hospitals, administration, teaching and research.

The total cost of these medical services is about $70 million a year. Treatment at all public hospitals is free, as is the provision of surgical appliances. Patients attending private hospitals have a proportion of their fees paid, at a flat daily rate; similar payments are made for patients in private maternity hospitals. (Virtually all births take place in hospital.) In the same way, a standard fee is paid as a proportion of the costs of services provided by doctors in private practice; the patient must pay the remainder. For general practitioners the present State fee is $1.25 for services provided during normal working hours and $2.00 for night, weekend, or holiday services. On average, the patient may pay an additional $2.00 to visit a doctor in his surgery and $2.50 for a home visit (extra outside normal working hours; most doctors still make home visits). All prescribed pharmaceuticals are provided free by registered pharmacists, who receive a payment from the State for each prescription dispensed.

Other health services are provided by private bodies, though often with government assistance. Advice on child-rearing, for example, is provided by the independent Plunket Society, which operates clinics in most towns and suburbs and also has a series of special *Karitane* hospitals for more difficult cases. The Department of Health nurses visit schools to make checks, and camps for convalescent and problem children are provided by the Health Camps Board, part of whose costs are met by the annual sale of health stamps on which there is a levy of 1 cent above the prescribed postal rate. Dental services for the general public are provided by private practitioners, whose fees for persons aged under sixteen are met by the State. For pre- and primary school children, however, there is a School Dental Service staffed by specially trained dental nurses at clinics located in the grounds of most primary schools.

There is continuing concern in New Zealand, as elsewhere, about the quality and quantity of the medical services provided. At present, for example, there is some concern that the country's health services are declining relative to those in some other countries, that hospital waiting lists are too long for non-urgent operations, and that many areas are poorly provided with services, notably doctors. The last problem is particularly pressing in country areas (though it is often also common in new suburbs), where the only doctor for a large area has a hard task. Many districts find it difficult to obtain, and to retain, practitioners, and several seek widely, at home and abroad, for long periods without success. To assist the worst affected areas, the Department of Health has defined special districts for which it provides the doctor with a salary, a car allowance, and a free house. Other schemes have been devised to give doctors more assistance and to free them from more trivial tasks, but the general problem of access to a general practitioner is not easily solved in many areas. To counter the long hospital waiting lists, and also to avoid the impersonality of the often large public hospitals, many people are now joining medical insurance societies, which give special rates to groups organised by employers and trade unions. For a small premium, which is tax deductible, individuals can obtain cover for themselves and their dependants which provides financial assistance, at standard rates, for certified visits to general practitioners and needed stays in private hospitals.

One area of medical services in which New Zealand is relatively poorly provided concerns family planning. The volunteer Family Planning Association has a clinic in most towns and general practitioners give advice; one consequence of this is the high proportion of New Zealand women—relative to those in other countries—taking the contraceptive pill. However, there has been no sex education in schools—indeed, in primary schools, discussion of sex can lead to instant dismissal for the teacher. Contraceptives are not widely available in supermarkets, for example. And perhaps as consequences of factors such as these, about one birth in seven occurs outside wedlock, as do about half of all first conceptions. Many of these conceptions may, however, occur within stable *de facto* relationships, particularly within the Maori population which is responsible for a large proportion of them. Concern is frequently expressed at the rising rates of extra-nuptial conceptions and births, but much of this trend is a statistical illusion, as Maori data have been included since 1961 only. Nevertheless, the rates are high in world terms. About one-third of all extra-nuptial births provide children for adoption (around 2,500 annually); one-quarter stay with both parents, and a further quarter (though the proportion is rising rapidly) stay with the mother.

THE BIRACIAL SOCIETY

Most descriptions of New Zealand life, in this and other books, tend to treat the population as a single society and to ignore the differences between the pakeha majority and the eight per cent who are members of the Maori race. One of the pakeha New Zealander's proudest boasts, and one that is justified in relation to the situation in many other countries, concerns the absence of racial discrimination and prejudice. In part, this reflects on the degree of spatial mixing of the two groups at different times. Race relations were generally bad in the first decades after the Treaty of Waitangi was signed because the Maori had a commodity—land—which the pakeha wanted. Once the dispute was settled—in the pakeha's favour—conflict subsided because the Maori retreated from contact with their 'conquerors'. Slowly Maori society was rebuilt, largely from within but with the aid of, in particular, pakeha medicine, and it has been rejuvenated in recent decades. The rapid population growth has been too great for the rural areas to support, however, so the Maori have been moving, in considerable numbers, to the towns and cities. Here they have come into contact with pakeha society again, and problems have emerged—though it must be stressed once more that these are by no means as serious as with the aborigines in Australia, the Negroes in the United States, or the coloured immigrants in Great Britain.

The basic problem is that of cultural conflict between Maori and pakeha, which introduces the need for policies which will ensure mutual accommodations. There are divergences at present both in economic and social spheres. In the former, pakeha aspirations, though tempered by the humanitarianism of the welfare state, clearly reflect the capitalist ethic with its stress on personal accumulation of wealth—and thereby power and status —allied with national economic growth. Maori society, on the other hand, has a much stronger basis of communal rather than individual wealth, and reciprocity rather than market exchange characterises many economic dealings. Thus, the extended family is the basic Maori social unit; the nuclear family is the common building-block of pakeha society.

Maori culture has been much changed by prolonged contact with the pakeha, yet it is still alive and developing new forms, many of which not surprisingly reflect the contact. Thus there is little doubt that a policy of assimilation, by which the Maori would be totally absorbed into pakeha (Kiwi) society and lose all cultural identity, is neither desirable nor feasible. Nor is it likely that the two societies will blend, with a mixture being the end result. And since separate development is not feasible or, except in very rare cases, demanded, then some form of racial integration must be pursued.

Integration involves cultural pluralism, with each group defining for itself which aspects of its heritage it wishes to retain. Unfortunately, where the groups are spatially mixed, as is increasingly the case in New Zealand, it is often difficult for such a policy to be administered. The result is usually that the majority attempts to determine in which spheres of life the minority must be assimilated, and in which it can retain its identity. In New Zealand, this has come to mean that, particularly in the towns and cities, the Maori must conform to pakeha norms in attitudes to work and property; it is pakeha law and order which prevails. On the other hand, the Maori is allowed to retain certain distinctive social customs; indeed he is encouraged to do so, so that pakeha society may put the 'noble savage' on public display— as at international festivals or on royal visits—and thereby indicate the success of the biracial state.

Pakehas have shown a surge of interest in Maori society in recent years; some of this is altruistic, some paternalistic. Many of the comparisons adduced have not suggested equality for the two groups, within a general New Zealand society. Maoris, for example, have life expectancies ten years or more shorter than those of their pakeha contemporaries; their infant mortality rate is twice that of pakeha children, their susceptibility to diseases such as TB is at least ten times greater, and they live in more crowded and less sanitary conditions. The arrest rate for Maoris is twice that of pakehas, a circumstance often partly associated with the Maori concept of communal property, but no doubt more related to Maori alienation in the large cities. More importantly, Maoris are much more likely to be found guilty, a difference which is apparently related to their ignorance of the procedures of pakeha justice and their inability to obtain (or even to realise they need) legal assistance. In education, the ratio of university graduation for pakehas is at least eight times that for Maoris; in work, Maoris are much more likely to be found in lower-status, lower-paid occupations.

These cultural differences suggest the operation of racial prejudice and discrimination in New Zealand. Some of it is based on economic differences between pakeha and Maori; the denial of rental property to Maoris, for example, is probably more frequently based on fears for the fabric because it will be used, temporarily at least, by a large and changing 'family', than on prejudice *per se*. Much of the discriminating behaviour is based on popular stereotypes of the Maori—stereotypes which it seems the Maori themselves have come largely to accept, many of which are probably not true. Thus it is widely accepted that Maoris are lackadaisical at and often absent from work, happy-go-lucky, sporting, and members of large families. What is less frequently accepted is that they are generally shy, especially in pakeha company, and frequently distrustful of pakeha motives; thus they appear to be hostile rather than casually friendly. But it is the stereotypes on which people act, and the stereotypes seem to be generally held, by those with plenty of contact with Maoris and those with little or none, and treatment is accorded to people who, it is believed by many, are in many ways not too far from the culturally primitive state which they occupied when the pakeha arrived.

Most pakeha are paternalistic and superior towards the Maori, therefore, while admitting that there are 'good Maoris'—those who conform to the pakeha ethos. Discrimination occurs, notably in accommodation; prejudice is displayed, as in derogatory remarks and the identification of a Maori (or other Polynesian) by his race, in newspaper reports of, for example, crimes and court appearances. Insensitivity is shown by the refusals of most pakeha to learn even the rudiments of the Maori language, a refusal which is reflected in the paucity of Maori language teaching in New Zealand's schools. (This is now being slowly altered.)

The cultural conflict between Maori and pakeha has in part been translated into an inter-generation conflict within Maori society. Older Maori generations have resisted integration, with many members preferring separate social and economic existences. Younger generations, however, have accepted some pakeha attitudes, such as the need for education, but this tends to alienate them from their kin. Some are able to endure this, and enter Kiwi society, either as integrated Maori or as assimilated New Zealanders; others find the stress of the contradictory pulls of the two societies too great, resulting in alienation and conflict —as displayed in the increasing crime rates and the growth of Maori 'gangs'.

In parts of New Zealand, most particularly the burgeoning Auckland urban area, immigration of other Polynesians is creating a multiracial rather than a biracial society. This gives to Auckland a cosmopolitan character which clearly distinguishes it from other New Zealand cities. It also is introducing further problems of cultural conflict, since relations are often strained among the various island groups. Some Pacific Islanders come to New Zealand as citizens; others come as visitors and as temporary workers. Many of them suffer considerable discrimination because of their ignorance of New Zealand society; some who come on visitors' permits but who remain as workers are subjected to many indignities because of their illegal status. In both housing and employment, many islanders suffer.

Compared with many countries with sizeable 'racial' minorities, New Zealand rates highly for its record on race relations. The humanitarian theme of much of the country's history extends to the attitude of most of its pakeha settlers to the Maori inhabitants, even though this was often paternalistic. But as the Maori and pakeha alike become more aware of the inequalities between them, the record of race relations is being subjected to greater scrutiny; the problem of how to remove the inequalities, while not extinguishing the cultural differences, is exercising the country's ingenuity.

4

How They Work

GRASSLAND farming is the backbone of New Zealand's economy; on it the whole prosperity of the society is structured. The prices at wool auctions within New Zealand; the returns from meat sales; the agreed volume and price of dairy produce exports to the EEC; these are the barometers of current prosperity and are major topics of debate, in Parliament, pub and parlour. A fall in receipts on all of the major primary exports—meat, wool, butter, cheese—brings a major economic depression, as in the early 1930s; a fall in income from one can cause a recession—as with wool prices in 1967—or attempts to restructure an industry—as with dairying in the last few years; a boom in sales, of course, brings great wealth quickly, as during the Korean War.

While the bush was being cleared and farms established, agriculture and pastoralism occupied a considerable proportion of the workforce. Now that the country is broken in, however, a major characteristic of farming is its small labour force and the very high productivity of labour. Some eleven per cent of the workforce are in farming. There are about 62,000 separate holdings—averaging 303 hectares each—and on average only two full-time workers on each.

The size of the farming workforce suggests an economy in which this small proportion supports the majority, but this is very much an exaggeration as many urban residents are part of the agricultural economy. There are, for example, about 23,000 freezing workers, processing meat, and 6,000 dairy factory employees; much of the work for the 7,000 watersiders involves handling agricultural exports. In addition, efficiency of labour

78

on farms is exaggerated. Machinery, which is fabricated and serviced in the towns and villages and in some cases operated by urban dwellers, is extensively used (farmers invested $61 million on capital equipment during 1971–2), and many farm tasks are contracted out, notably sheep shearing—to travelling gangs—and the application of fertiliser and grass-seed. And much of the work in the economy's commercial sector—the banks and lawyers' offices, the accounting firms and stock and station agencies—is directly or indirectly associated with farming, so it is not surprising that changes in agricultural prices rapidly reverberate throughout society.

New Zealand is often stereotyped as one huge farm, Britain's antipodean grassland. In many respects this is so, although improved grassland covers only forty-five per cent of the country. Most parts of both islands share the fortunate characteristic of a year-round temperate climate which means no seasonal absence of grass-growth, although spring and, to a lesser extent, early autumn are the main periods of growth. But the farming scene displays many regional varieties, reflecting climatic, geologic and pedologic differences.

The biggest difference in farm types is between the small dairy farms and the large sheep stations. The former are concentrated in the milder, more humid districts of the west coasts of both islands, areas which are less susceptible to seasonal drought and have relatively flat land. The Taranaki and Waikato districts are the main dairying areas, followed by Northland and Manawatu. Farms of 80 hectares, carrying 120 cattle, are typical of the better areas; they are often run by one man, who can milk that many cows twice daily and perform other tasks about his holding only by using advanced technology, notably in his milking-shed. Except near to the towns, where dairy farmers contract to provide a year-round supply of milk, payment is for the milk's butterfat content since most of it is used in the co-operative dairy factories, for the manufacture of butter, cheese and an ever-widening range of by-products, such as milk powder and biscuits. Jersey cattle have dominated the herds because of their high butterfat output, but recently there has been considerable diversification towards the production of dairy beef (by raising the calves and fattening them for the freezing-works rather than slaughtering them after birth); for this dual purpose, the Friesian has been proving more suitable.

New Zealand's dairy farming has evolved its own methods of tenure, which both assist new farmers build up their capital and move towards farm ownership and allow owners to avoid the tedium of the daily milking. Share-milking involves a variety of agreements, whose form is controlled by law, in which the land's owners take a portion of the tenant's income in return for use of the farm. Income is usually split 50–50 if the tenant provides the cows and does all maintenance, 61–39 if the owner provides the herd, and 71–29 if the owner both provides the herd and does all maintenance, the tenant merely milking and feeding the cows.

In contrast to the small dairy farms are the large sheep stations, most of them in the South Island 'high country' on the flanks of the Southern Alps. Some of these are more than 20,000 hectares in area; most are on land leased from the state, though the small area around the homestead may be owned by the farmer. Formerly, these stations employed many men, who lived in a small settlement compound around the owner-manager's homestead. With the introduction of machinery and of the contracting-out of many tasks, however, workforce requirements have fallen; for example the use of small motor cycles has reduced the need for shepherds, who used to move on horse or by foot and may have spent weeks living in small huts well away from the homestead. Those left on the station live a relatively lonely existence, though few are more than two hours' drive from a town and many farmers maintain an urban dwelling; in such circumstances, however, it is often difficult to obtain hired labour.

On these stations the sheep, often in flocks of 10,000 or more, range freely over the hillsides during summer. They are mustered perhaps only twice a year, once for shearing and the other in autumn, for culling out the surplus stock, which are sent either to a freezing works or to farms on lower country for fattening. During the winter, stock are kept in the better, low-lying pastures in the valleys near to the homesteads, areas which are carefully sub-divided into 'paddocks' to ensure efficient use of the available feed. Many of these sheep stations are suffering from extensive erosion of their hillside pastures, a result of earlier over-stocking and the depredations of rabbits and other pests. Increasingly, therefore, land is being 'retired' for conservation purposes, to protect not only the slopes themselves but also the plains areas fed by the rivers draining the high country stations. Much work is being done on the best use for this upland area also, and there is a trend towards the joint running of sheep and of beef cattle, particularly Herefords; wool remains the major source of income, however.

The high country sheep stations, and the large upland farms of the North Island—which also are now running beef cattle with sheep—are not independent units in the farming system. In the rolling country between mountains and coast, on the 'downs' and plains, are livestock-fattening farms, many of which obtain stock from the stations higher up. Meat is their main source of income, breeding of stock a major sideline. Such farms, of between 400 and 2,000 hectares, running both sheep and beef cattle, are perhaps most typical of the New Zealand scene.

Within this general matrix of farm types, whose form is determined by local topography and climate, are a few small, specialised farming districts. Most cultivation of grain crops takes place on the dry east coast of the South Island; here there was a 'wheat bonanza' in the 1880s, but New Zealand now has to import grain in most years, and the amount of area sown depends very much on the government-controlled price. The flat, extensive Canterbury Plains, which are warm and dry in late summer/early autumn, produce most of the wheat crop, though there is no monoculture and most farmers obtain considerable income from livestock; further south, in Otago and Southland, are the main areas of oats and barley cultivation.

Many of the urban areas were sited on, or adjacent to, the country's most fertile alluvial soils, which are used for the production of vegetables for the local market. Some areas serve the whole of New Zealand with a particular product—an area near Oamaru, for example, provides most of the brussels sprouts cultivated. The development of vegetable canning and freezing industries has been based on these soils, particularly on the Heretaunga Plains outside Hastings and also near to Gisborne and Christchurch. Hops and tobacco are grown near Motueka, much of the production being processed locally.

Fruit-growing is also common on these fertile soils, providing further inputs for the canneries and freezers. The Nelson and Hawke's Bay areas are the main apple producers, though there are commercial orchards outside many cities. Christchurch is an important centre for raspberry cultivation; the inland basins of Central Otago provide most of New Zealand's plums, apricots and cherries, although here the farmers must be ever-vigilant for the potentially destructive late frosts. The sub-tropical north of the North Island—Northland, the Bay of Plenty and Poverty Bay—is a source of considerable quantities of citrus fruit, passion fruit, tamarillos (tree tomatoes), and Chinese gooseberries (Kiwi fruit); citrus trees flourish in protected spots in individual gardens as far south as Christchurch. Finally, there are more than 300 vineyards, producing for wine production (the local white wines are considered to be high standard). The Auckland area has most vineyards, followed by the dry east coast areas of the North Island; vineyards have recently been established in the dry and sunny, though frost-prone, north of the South Island.

Farmland productivity has been achieved, and is maintained, by considerable hard work, backed by investment in machinery and methods, each of which in turn is the subject of much research. Of the 26·9 million hectares in New Zealand, 17·4 million are in occupied farms, 13·1 million of them under grass. Two-thirds of all grassland (one-third of the whole area of the country) is improved; following the removal of native bush and tussock— by hard labour assisted by machinery and controlled burning— the land has been sown with exotic grasses and clovers. The latter are very important for 'fixing' nitrogen, and careful application of fertilisers—phosphates and lime in particular—stimulates their growth.

A very big boost to grassland management, especially in the high country, was the introduction in 1949 of aerial topdressing services. Small aircraft are now flown by about eighty operators, from some 8,000 grass airstrips, distributing 800,000 tons of fertilisers and lime, 1,000 tons of seed, seven million gallons of spray, and 4,000 tons of poison each year over about three million hectares of land. This involves 100,000 flying hours, broken up into many short flights of only a few minutes' duration as the pilots land, refill their sprays, take off and distribute, and return for more to what may be a hazardous and bumpy 'runway' which ends with a sheer drop over a precipice and has steep mountain walls on two sides. Not surprisingly there is an average of one accident a week—four for every 1,000 hours flown. The cost of the service is consequently high, and farmers tend to reduce the amount of topdressing when prices fall, but without it much upland pasture could not be maintained as productive grassland.

Not surprisingly, the importance of farming to New Zealand's economy means that there is a great deal of government involvement in the industry. The Department of Scientific and Industrial Research contains several divisions whose work is directly or indirectly related to agriculture; the Ministry of Agriculture runs several research stations; and the Lands and Survey Department is active in farm development. There are two agricultural colleges at which much research is undertaken and degrees and diplomas are offered in a range of subjects such as agricultural engineering and veterinary science, horticulture and land valuation, food technology and range management; one of these formed the basis for Massey University, at Palmerston North, and the other, Lincoln College, is a quasi-independent faculty of the University of Canterbury. In addition, there is the Ministry of Agriculture's farm advisory service, which is staffed by over a hundred graduates and keeps farmers informed of developments in the industry. There are daily radio and weekly TV programmes—at peak hours—for farmers.

Government invests much money in farming, in the irrigation schemes on the Canterbury Plains and in parts of Otago, for example, as well as community-controlled projects in fruit-growing districts. The water is charged for at a rate which will cover the capital cost in forty years. The Lands and Survey Department is active in opening up new areas for farming, particularly in Northland and Southland and on the Volcanic Plateau around Rotorua. Land is cleared and brought into production, houses and farm buildings are erected, fencing is put in and stock introduced, and the farm is then operated by department staff until it is economically viable. At that time it is sold, at attractive terms, to a 'new farmer' who has been selected usually by ballot from among applicants who have attended training programmes. In this way, land that individuals could not afford to 'break in' is made fertile, young farmers are given a good start in an increasingly expensive occupation to enter, and the economy continues to expand: at present, enough land is either under development or awaiting it for about 1,500 new farms to be established. Similar projects are undertaken by the department for the Department of Maori Affairs, setting up viable farms (perhaps co-operatively operated) on communal land.

Farming is a complex and risky operation, and its future depends on difficult decisions concerning types of enterprises, to be made not only by the farmers themselves but also by those who hand them the large sums needed for development—the banks and the stock and station agents. With guaranteed markets and with prices rising in line with general living costs, New Zealand's efficient farmers, and hence New Zealand, are prosperous. But with Britain's entry into the EEC and the general trend in prices for primary products, both of these props are being attacked. Always before, there has been a boom after every recession, but it is far from clear that 'she'll be right' again this time. Consequently, after a period of procrastination in the early 1960s, there is now a frenzy of activity aimed at diversification of

---

New Zealanders watching their favourite sport, Rugby Union football; a match between the national side (the All Blacks) and the President's XV at Athletic Park, Wellington in August 1973.
Horse-racing is the other major crowd-puller in New Zealand, as at Addington Raceway, Christchurch on the New Zealand Metropolitan Trotting Club's Cup Day.

products and markets, while continuing the search for greater productivity. Very clearly there are world shortages in foodstuffs, but just as clearly, New Zealand's foodstuffs are expensive, if not luxury, items in those countries with the greatest need. There will, it seems, be an almost permanent problem of farm prices in the future.

FORESTRY

Export of native woods to Australia was New Zealand's first major international trading venture. Extraction of the timber was far from scientific, however, and many areas and species, such as the Northland Kauri forests, were almost completely destroyed. Bush-clearing removed much more valuable native forest. Nevertheless, nearly a quarter of the country's total area is still forested. Much of this is mountainous land, however, in high rainfall areas; here the dense bush is unmerchantable but performs a very valuable task in regulating run-off.

Forestry is growing in importance as a provider of export income. It now employs over 6,000 persons, in two types of work. The first is protection forestry, which aims to maintain and improve the upland tree cover, thereby protecting the land resource

---

Surf Carnivals are where teams of voluntary patrolmen compete, both in lifesaving methods and in drill. The marchpast at the National Lifesaving Championships, held at Titahi Bay, Wellington in 1968, is shown here.
A watersport available to only a few is jetboating. The jetboat was developed in New Zealand for use on the country's shallow, braided rivers, such as the Waimakariri, shown here in its gorge inland of Christchurch. Jetboats are used in a variety of tasks, including bush rescues, and form a profitable export line.

lower down (by reducing soil erosion and flood hazards). Such work involves not only research about, and conservation of the tree resource, but also control of the noxious animals, notably deer and wild pigs, whose dietary requirements severely inhibit forest regeneration. Provision of forests for recreation is involved also, in the large National and State Forest Parks, where both exotic and indigenous species co-exist, and also the Forest Sanctuaries, which house indigenes only.

Commercial forestry, the second type, is one of New Zealand's most rapidly growing industries. Some of it uses indigenous timber, but much of this is of poor quality and is difficult to work. Three-quarters of the felled timber comes from large forests of exotic trees established in the 1920s and 1930s. Experiment had shown that New Zealand's climate was ideal for certain pine species, notably *pinus radiata*, which would mature in about thirty years only. Over a quarter of a million hectares were planted in the ten years from 1926, more than half by the State, which provided much relief for the unemployed in this way (albeit usually in fairly harsh and primitive conditions). By far the largest of these forests mantle the Volcanic Plateau in the central North Island where the land, because of a cobalt deficiency not then understood, was unsuited for farming.

With the maturation of these forests, and a six-fold increase in the amount of exotic timber felled, industrial complexes based on timber use have been established in the last two decades. (Before then, small sawmills, most with only short life expectancy because of a limited resource, characterised the industry.) Some 32,000 people are now employed in wood processing; many of them live in the new towns established in the central North Island since 1950. The State forests are exploited by the Tasman Pulp and Paper Company, in which the government holds a major interest; its main plant is at the new town of Kawerau (built by the government), and its logging operations are run from a smaller new town of Murupara, at the head of a railway specially constructed for log movements. The other major company—New Zealand's largest—is New Zealand Forest Products, which has its own forests west of the State blocks (north of Lake Taupo); its large mill is at Kinleith, near the new town of Tokoroa. As more forests mature, further industrial projects will follow; present plans are for plants at Napier and at Nelson, and planting—both replacement and new—continues.

Forest products now earn about seven per cent of export income. Pulp and paper, and logs are exported in almost equal value, with most of the former going to Australia and of the latter to Japan. This growth has produced massive expansion at the port of Tauranga, which handles the largest export cargoes by volume. A new rail link is being forged, by way of a tunnel through the Kaimai Ranges, to speed up the movement.

MINING

New Zealand is rich in land resources for farming, but, unlike neighbouring Australia, poor in mineral resources. Most minerals exist in New Zealand, but usually in small, low grade, and often almost inaccessible deposits. Gold is plentiful, of course, both in seams and in river gravels. Its discovery was a major catalyst to immigration and settlement in the South Island during the 1860s, and approximately 27 million ounces have been won. Today, however, the costs of mining and dredging are prohibitive; one dredge is still operating in the rivers of the South Island's West Coast, producing about $400,000 worth each year.

Coal is the only mineral presently mined in any quantity, although production and consumption have been rapidly declining of late. There are about ninety mines operating, employing about 2,000 persons and producing two million tons a year. The State runs twenty-five of the mines, at an annual loss of over $5 million. There are two main fields, producing bituminous coal on the West Coast of the South Island and sub-bituminous coal in the North Island's Waikato district; several other very small fields are worked in both islands.

The common image of coal mining is of a despoiled landscape in a 'black country' but New Zealand's coalfields certainly do not fit this. On the Buller field, around Westport, for example, are a number of small mines, many located deep in the bush and making but a small blot on the landscape. In the northern part of the field, along the coast north of Westport, the mines are 1,000 metres or more above sea level, reached by roads up the precipitous front slopes of raised shorelines. Settlement was initially alongside the mines, in very bleak environments some parts of which were above the tree line. Such 'villages' are now largely deserted and the miners commute daily from coastal townships, where they enjoy a sub-tropical winter.

Coal usage has fallen in recent years with the removal of all steam engines from the railways and the transfer to oil for many heating purposes. The main use is now for power generation, especially with the coal won from the opencast Waikato mines. One large thermal station alongside the Waikato River consumes 700,000 tons annually, and another is planned. Future developments hinge on the present uncertainty about oil prices; new power stations are being planned but it has not been decided whether they will use coal. Possibilities of exporting Buller coal to Japan are frequently raised but there are harbour problems on the coast there; closure of more mines on the West Coast, however, will bring social and economic problems to what is already New Zealand's 'depressed area'.

Apart from ubiquitous sands and gravels which are quarried for construction and roading uses, plus the widespread lime deposits used for agriculture and cement, the only minerals being worked in quantity at present are the ironsands on the beaches of the west coast, North Island. An integrated steelworks was built in the 1960s, with considerable government aid, to use these; its location south of Auckland gives it access to coal and limestone available nearby and to the nation's largest industrial market.

POWER

Hydro-electricity provides eighty-five per cent of all New Zealand's power. The rivers flowing from the mountain backbone, especially in the higher and wetter South Island, provide considerable potential along their steep gradients; the glacially-formed basins, often occupied by natural lakes and separated by narrow rocky gorges, provide excellent locales for manipulation of the flow of water and generation of the electricity. Thus many of the rivers are dammed, creating strings of artificial lakes on, for example, the Waitaki in the South Island, and the Waikato —which has eight installations—in the North Island.

Per capita consumption of electricity is increasing fast, and this trend is likely to continue. The potential for further power schemes is small, however. A very large development is progressing in the upper Waitaki basin, involving construction of large canals for the transfer of water between lakes, but most future schemes are likely to be small-yielding. The paucity of the resource is being exacerbated by the growing environmental concern about large landscape-modifying schemes. A campaign against the raising of Lake Manapouri, in the Fiordland National Park, which raged throughout the 1960s, peaking at the end of the decade, has been the major conservation effort. Successive government agreements with Comalco stipulated that the latter would build an aluminium smelter near Invercargill (using Australian bauxite) in return for cheap power from Manapouri. The contracts concerned supply capacity and required raising the lake; the campaign eventually led to a decision against raising, but rather to maintain the normal range of levels. At present there is considerable controversy—some of it political—over plans to develop the last major river resource, the Clutha in the South Island. Present proposals involve six dams and an investment of $400 million; unlike other schemes, settled areas are threatened, including part of a town and hundreds of hectares of orchards.

A major problem concerning hydro-electricity is that whereas much of the production and remaining potential is in the South Island, the growing demand is in the north of the North Island. Transmission lines have been built north from the Waitaki River, including a twenty-five-mile cable under Cook Strait. This transfer of power annoys many protagonists of South Island's regional development claims; occasional threats are made to cut the cable and secede!

Geothermal energy provides half of the electricity not generated by hydro-power: this is produced at Waitakei, just north of Lake Taupo, where turbines are driven by natural steam which is harnessed through a complex of bores and pipes that, with the clouds of steam hanging in the valley, creates a 'science fiction' type of landscape. Unfortunately, the potential for further power from this source is not great, and only one more field will be developed during the next decade. In the future, therefore, more use will be made of fossil fuels. Until recently, it was intended that all new generating stations, with the exception of one now being constructed on the Waikato River, should be oil-driven, but the rapid price rise for that commodity since late 1973 has caused reconsideration of the use of the extensive coal resources, and more stations driven by this power source are now likely.

New Zealand has no large, proven oil deposits. A small field has been producing at New Plymouth since 1911, providing the material for a locally-retailed brand of petrol, but extensive exploration in Taranaki and elsewhere has not unearthed any exploitable fields. Natural gas in workable quantities has been discovered however. That from Kapuni, in Taranaki, has been piped to Auckland and Wellington since 1970; a large offshore field, Maui, is now being developed, with many problems because of the deep, rough seas. To date, town gas from coal has not been widely manufactured and distributed—there are just over 100,000 consumers—but it is hoped that natural gas will be widely used, both in domestic and industrial appliances and in electricity generation.

FISHING

As a coastal nation, it is not surprising that considerable quantities of fish are eaten in New Zealand, though not as much per person as in Great Britain and much less than in Japan. Indeed, the offshore resource is poorly exploited by locals (some 3,000 boats land about 40,000 tons a year), and greater catches are undoubtedly made by the Japanese and Russian fleets which are commonly present just outside New Zealand's territorial waters. A major role of the New Zealand Navy is to patrol the fishing limit, over which incursions by overseas boats are quite frequent.

Marine delicacies are a frequent element of New Zealand diet, apart from the ubiquitous fish and chips. Oyster beds in Foveaux Strait (between Stewart and the South Island) provide over 100,000 sacks a year (the industry is closely controlled by a licensing system during a defined season); on a world scale, the oysters are sold at very reasonable prices. (They are also sold, deep fried with chips, in most take-away shops.) Rock oysters are plentiful around the Auckland peninsula and crayfish (rock lobsters) are common on many parts of the coast. During the late 1960s there was a crayfish boom in the waters around the lonely Chatham Islands some 850 kilometres east of Christchurch (there is a permanent population of 700), with most of the tails being exported to the United States: it is feared, however, that the field has been over-fished, despite regulations on the size of fish that can be taken. Finally, a much appreciated local delicacy is whitebait, caught in the mouths of many rivers, especially those of the South Island's west coast.

INDUSTRIES AND SERVICES

New Zealand's industrial scene is one of a multiplicity of small factories interspersed with a few large modern plants. There are some 10,500 factories, which on average employ twenty-five persons, each of whom produces $15,000 worth of goods annually, yielding a surplus of about $1,000 to the manufacturer. More than sixty per cent of all plants employ less than ten persons, but, on the other hand, forty per cent of all employees work at factories which employ a hundred or more.

There are two traditional sections of the country's industrial economy, with one processing primary products for export and the other providing consumer goods for the local market. In the former sector are the meat freezing and the dairy factories. Nearly every region has a large freezing works—there are thirty-three in all—at which livestock are slaughtered and prepared for the refrigerated hold. Most operate throughout the year, but killing peaks during the summer when the labour force might be doubled—providing seasonal work for many, including both students and itinerant labourers. The average workforce exceeds 500 men, in marked contrast to the smaller dairy factories, for which average employment in the 200 plants is twenty. Many of these plants are co-operatives, established and run by the farmers who provide the butterfat. A large number of very small roadside and small settlement factories have been closed in the last two decades, and there are now several very large, computer-controlled factories. The precursor of this change was the introduction of bulk milk collection by tanker in the late 1940s, which enables factories to get the perishable raw material from a much wider area than when churn, cart and lorry were the means of transport.

Industries producing consumer goods from local resources were established in many towns from the earliest years of settlement. Flourmills and sawmills, brickworks and breweries, bakeries and tanneries; these and a variety of other small enterprises could be found in most places. A few have survived, having grown into large modern plants in most cases, but most have disappeared, unable to compete with the large firms which first captured the markets of the big cities and then successfully competed against their weaker small-town counterparts.

As the New Zealand economy grew, so it became possible to replace imported goods by locally-produced items; in many cases these were, and still are, based on imported components and materials, for the country has neither a large enough market for many of the very specialised processes nor the raw materials necessary for the basic heavy industries of a highly industrialised nation. The largest component of this sector is concerned with transport equipment, with plants ranging in size from the sixteen assemblers of motor cars (average employment 120) to the 3,000 repair establishments which average seven workers each.

The difference between large and small factories is highlighted in their ownership patterns. The aspirations to 'be one's own boss' is as strong in this sector of the economy as in farming and retailing, and many of the small establishments represent an individual running his own business. Some survive as small firms, many fail; a few are 'rags to riches' success stories spawning industrial empires, as was the case with the late Sir James Wattie. In contrast to the 'self-made man' is the foreign-owned establishment, which is probably among the largest in the country. (Half of all foreign-owned establishments employ more than 200 persons; foreign ownership is defined as firms with more than one-quarter of the equity held overseas.) The following statistics indicate the increasing role of foreign-ownership of New Zealand industry, a cause of considerable local concern.

	Size of Foreign-Owned Sector 1963-4		Growth Rate % 1955-6/1963-4	
		% of NZ Total	Foreign-Owned	All Industry
Number of Establishments	489	5	82	10
Number of Employees	40,000	20	73	26
Output ($m)	495	26	107	65
Value Added ($m)	200	26	169	90
Manufacturers' Surplus ($m)	61	32	349	122
Value Land/ Buildings ($m)	106	25	163	122
Value Plant/ Machinery ($m)	86	35	116	68

Of the various industrial sectors, foreign ownership is greatest in vehicle assembly, the manufacture of electrical machinery, beverage and tobacco manufacture, and the production of chemicals and rubberware. Nearly half of the employment so controlled is by British companies, with a third by Australian and about a tenth by American and other nationalities. The American firms are much more frequently wholly overseas-owned.

The poor development of the industrial sector reflects both the small size of the New Zealand market and the country's 'dependent' position in the British colonial economic system. Since the 1930s, however, successive governments have made great efforts to increase and diversify the nation's industries. Some of their ventures, such as a cotton mill at Nelson, have failed, and others have had many problems, but there have been notable successes also, in the use of both local resources—as at the Waiuku steelworks and the Volcanic Plateau papermills—and imported materials. Some of the most spectacular developments are in the urban areas at the two extremities of the country; Whangarei has the only oil refinery, plus fertiliser, cement, and glass works; Invercargill has the large aluminium smelter.

Import replacement industrialisation is concentrated largely into the main urban areas, in particular Auckland whose rapid population growth in recent decades is witness to the great industrial expansion there. That urban area, and its environs, now has almost a third of the country's factories and jobs; the Wellington area has a fifth, and Christchurch a sixth. Auckland's industries are widely based; other places are very much more specialised—Wellington/Hutt in transport equipment, for example, and Christchurch in rubber and plastic products. And the smaller towns are characterised in the most part by small engineering firms, catering for the local farmers' needs, with perhaps a few clothing factories employing women. Local resources may produce a speciality, as with the tobacco industry at Motueka. Almost all of these factories produce exclusively for the local market (indeed, in the smaller towns, for their regional markets only), and there are few which export in any quantity. There are notable exceptions, such as the Hamilton light aircraft producer and the Christchurch manufacturers of the locally-invented jetboat, but overseas markets are difficult to develop and maintain from this small and isolated country. There are many government incentives to export, however, and some commentators feel that New Zealand's future prosperity will need it to grow as a 'Switzerland of the South Pacific'.

One final, slowly changing feature of New Zealand industry is that it is labour intensive and relatively inefficient in its use of fixed assets. Shift work is not common in the urban areas and so, with the ethos of the long weekend, most factories work a five-day, forty-hour week. With the introduction of expensive technology and the increasing cost of labour, this pattern will certainly change, but at present the approach is relatively relaxed.

Half of the New Zealand labour force is employed in services, keeping the wheels of commerce moving and ensuring the distribution of goods into and out of the country. Commerce alone employs 200,000—forty per cent of them women—and a further 250,000 are employed in various business and community services, including government. These service industries are even more concentrated in the urban areas than are the manufacturing plants; in Auckland, over forty per cent of males work other than in factories, as do three-quarters of the female members of the workforce.

FOREIGN TRADE

New Zealand's dependence on foreign trade for the inhabitants' prosperity cannot be over-stressed. The value of trade per head is one of the highest in the world, and export earnings make up about one-fifth of the national income. Thus individual prosperity is very much tied up with the prices for the country's main exports, both as direct payments to the producer and as indications of how much can be spent on needed imports, not only of consumer goods but also of equipment and materials necessary for the strengthening of the economy.

There are two major characteristics of this trade; the 'dependence' on a few primary product exports, and the dependence on a single market source of supply. The primary products have dominated annual export manifestoes for a century, though in varying proportions among themselves. Meat, butter, cheese, and wool have accounted for as much as ninety-one per cent of total exports by value; at present they comprise eighty per cent, as a result of diversification made possible by growth of the forest product industries and the small, but growing, volume of manufactured exports. In return, New Zealand now buys capital goods, materials and components for local fabrication, and consumer items, as well as some foods (such as sugar) and the much-needed oil. Half of all imports enter through the port of Auckland.

The country on which New Zealand has depended for so long in the international market place is the United Kingdom, although this dependence has been rapidly altered in recent years. In 1910, the peak year of the 'imperial economic link', Britain took eighty-four per cent of all exports, by value, and provided sixty-two per cent of all imports; the respective percentages were fifty-one and thirty-six in 1965, and are thirty and twenty-eight at present. This diversion of trade from the traditional partner results from the wide search for new markets, much of whose intensity was a consequence of Britain's courtship of and eventual marriage with the European Economic Community. The United States now takes about one-fifth of all exports—almost all of it beef and veal—and Australia takes a tenth—the main commodity being newsprint; Japan is also a big buyer, in particular of timber, and great efforts are being made to develop meat markets there. Of the country's imports, Australia now provides nearly a quarter, including a wide range of metals, alloys and machinery; Japan and the United States both supply about one-tenth.

Because of the importance of trade, and trade development, to New Zealand's economy, it is not surprising that government is very active in this field. All exports are licenced, thereby ensuring government knowledge and control of the country's foreign exchange earnings, and it issues licences for imports according to its annual schedule. Exchange control is very tight. Trade promotion is actively pursued, through twenty-nine trade commissions, frequent trade missions, and intense activity at many trade fairs. One of the country's perennial problems has been its dependence on overseas shippers, notably the British Conference Lines, and its weak position in the determination of rates; like most small countries, New Zealand has to bear transport costs on both imports and exports. Producer boards have recently been active in seeking cheaper services, and in 1972 the government established a New Zealand Shipping Line to try and counter the problem.

INCOMES AND PURCHASING POWER

The incomes of most New Zealand wage and salary earners are subject to close control and constraint by government-created institutions, the most important of which is the Court of Arbitration, established as long ago as 1894. It comprises a Judge of the Supreme Court and one representative each of registered workers and employers. The Court comes into action when workers and employers in a particular industry or place fail to reach agreement. Their dispute goes first to a panel of assessors, chaired by a Conciliation Commissioner; if these do not agree, the case goes for final decision to the Court, which usually sets a minimum wage rate plus any relevant conditions. General wage orders may also be set by the Court, stipulating minimum wages for various categories (skilled etc) of work, for all workers, or introducing an across-the-board increase in wages. The wage awards which it makes are minima only; ruling rates may be considerably higher.

The facilities and procedures of the Court of Arbitration are available only to those trade unions registered with it; registration brings with it certain responsibilities, such as loss of the freedom to strike except in certain, very special, circumstances. Many occupations—notably the 'white-collar occupations'—are covered by other agreements. Government employees, for example, are presently awarded pay increases on the basis of regular surveys of the ruling rates in the private sector. Many of these awards—such as those for school-teachers—set mandatory salaries.

During periods of either recession or rapid inflation, governments often add to the wage-control legislation. In the depression of the 1930s, for example, State servants received across-the-board pay cuts and private employers were able to act similarly. At present, with rapid inflation, attempts are made, through stabilisation regulations, to limit the maximum wage increases; general wage orders with cost-of-living increases are allowed.

It is widely believed that there is much less variation in individual incomes in New Zealand than in most other countries, and this is almost certainly so, especially with after-tax incomes. The exact distribution of incomes is difficult to assess, however, because of the large number of self-employed persons and government beneficiaries (whose incomes are subject to tax). Of males employed at the time of the 1971 census, a quarter earned between $3,000–4,000 annually; over sixty per cent earned $2,200–5,000 a year, and only 16,000 of nearly 800,000 reported incomes exceeded $10,000. Among women, incomes of $1,000–1,800 were most common, with only 9,000 earning in excess of $4,000.

The relative equality of incomes can be illustrated in several ways. In every one of the census industrial classifications—mining, transport, business etc—the most common income category in 1971 was $3,000–3,999 for males. (There was, of course, a greater spread in some; over five per cent of those in business earned $10,000–15,000, but only one per cent of those in manufacturing.) In the manufacturing sector, the minimum weekly rates set by the Court of Arbitration in 1972 ranged from $49 for some construction workers to $116 for slaughtermen— but for fifty of the sixty-one published awards the minimum was between $50–70. Awards in service industries were generally lower. Half-yearly surveys of earnings for both ordinary and overtime are taken and published; the October 1972 averages were:

| | $ per Hour | | Hours Worked | |
	Ordinary Time	Overtime	Ordinary Time	Overtime
Forestry/Logging	1·823	2·878	38·2	2·6
Mining/Quarrying	2·109	2·785	36·9	6·7
Manufacturing	1·862	2·832	36·7	4·7
Construction	1·919	2·805	38·7	5·5
Retail	1·545	2·436	37·1	1·4
Transport/ Communications	1·981	3·057	38·4	4·6
Finance/ Insurance	2·129	2·730	37·0	0·6
Community/Business/ Government	2·090	2·645	36·8	1·2

The most disadvantaged, in both rates of pay and hours of work available, are those in shops and warehouses, but in general the variance is not great.

Income must be matched with expenditure patterns to assess the degree of equality fully, but for this data are difficult to obtain. Comparison of wage and price increases, however, shows that although New Zealand has experienced very rapid price increases in basic commodities during the last decade, purchasing power is increasing. For adult males, average wages increased by seventy-five per cent over the 1965–72 period, but because of price rises, the increase in real incomes was only twelve per cent. Most wage and salary earners have received such boosts, the main exception being those in the primary industries.

Survey data and general inferences suggest that the most disadvantaged groups in New Zealand are pensioners on fixed benefits and large, young families. The latter suffer most critically in the early years of their family cycle, especially if they are servicing a mortgage and the wife is not earning outside the home. There are also regional variations because awards are national but some components of living costs, notably those for housing, vary considerably. In times of labour shortage (very common in New Zealand), and especially in the booming industrial cities of the north, this often results in few people being paid only the award rate, so that new awards merely lift the relative floor for those in the 'depressed areas' whose bargaining power with employers is relatively weak.

Regular income does not take into account variations in personal assets. Only rough estimates of family and individual capital holdings are available, mainly from death duty returns. They indicate significant inequalities, some of them associated with age ('the younger, the poorer'). Of the total personal wealth, about one-fifth is held by only 20,000 individuals, and half by 100,000. But there are few who are very rich, by world standards: there are probably less than 200 millionaires and 1,000 holding more than $300,000. At the other extreme, poverty is even harder to define. On the society's general norms, however, it is suggested that as many as one-fifth of all families are 'struggling to make ends meet'; since many of these are large families, as many as 250,000 children may be involved.

TRADE UNIONS AND LABOUR

Trade unions were first legalised in 1878—by an Act which is still extant and occasionally used—but it was the 1894 Industrial Conciliation and Arbitration Act which fostered them, since it offered compulsory arbitration of all disputes for registered unions. As arbitration is compulsory for employers, the system ensures extensive protection of workers' rights, given the general sympathy of the Court of Arbitration to the 'dignity of labour'.

The IC&A Act at first applied only to workers in manufacturing industries, but its brief was widened early in the twentieth century. From 1936 to 1961, compulsory unionism existed, since all Court awards included a clause that employers could take on only union labour. (Compulsory unionism is still virtually the case.) At present, nearly 400,000 workers are represented by about 350 registered unions, many of which are small, referring to a specific trade in a specific place; it is perhaps a mark of the relative isolation of cities and towns in New Zealand that there are few large manufacturing unions. Outside the IC&A system are the white-collar workers, many of them in large national unions such as the Public Service Association (49,000 members) and the Post Office Association (29,000).

Most trade unions registered under the IC&A Act are members of the Federation of Labour, which has nineteen district Trade Councils plus a National Council and Executive, for which the President, and occasionally the Secretary, act as spokesmen. The Federation acts as a general representative for unions on a wide range of labour matters—including general wage orders and government proposals for legislation affecting workers—and also arbitrates on inter-union disputes. There are close ties, especially financial ones, between unions, the Federation and the Labour Party, though the strength of these bonds is often exaggerated; critics accuse the Labour Party of being merely a tool of the Federation, but there is often considerable strife between the two, especially when the Labour Party is in office as government.

———

Visitors on the shores of Waimangu Cauldron, the world's largest near-boiling body of water (just over four hectares), which is just south of Rotorua. Steam, much of it sulphorous, escapes from the mountainside also, giving an eerie feeling to tourists walking through the several miles of the valley.

One of the major contributions of the compulsory arbitration legislation has almost certainly been to keep down the number of strikes. There was, for example, no strike at all between 1894 and 1906; through the 1930s there was an average of about fifty a year, and a hundred a year in the fifties and sixties. Three major strike concentrations, marking notable worker-employer/ government confrontations, have occurred, in 1913, 1949–51, and since 1967. The first two were led by unions representing large workforces concentrated in a few places, such as miners, watersiders and freezing workers. Strikes by the latter two have caused much bitterness because of the country's dependence on them for export income (New Zealand watersiders have long had a poor reputation, reflected in the slow turn-round of ships). Thus the government soon becomes involved; in the 1951 waterfront stoppage troops were used to work the wharves and new, very punitive legislation was introduced to control strikers. One course of action available is for the government to deregister a union, thereby freezing its finances; new unions can then be set up and apply for registration, and the government can virtually set the terms of acceptance, and may itself generate the new union. The registration terms usually end the strike. Such procedures were used in 1951, and again in 1971, the latter to halt a

---

Young New Zealanders going to school in Christchurch, wearing the typical summer uniform. School patrols operated by senior pupils—though always supervised by either a parent or a teacher—are a common sight on city streets, as are the many bicycles.
A Maori concert party performing an action song, in front of typically carved and painted woodwork, interspersed with woven wall-hangings. Among the individuals whose pictures hang above the performers are two of the New Zealand Labour Party's most illustrious servants, Michael Joseph Savage, Prime Minister 1935–40 (third from left), and Walter Nash, Prime Minister 1957–60 (second from right).

potentially very damaging strike by seamen. Apart from these major confrontations, however, strikes are generally few and, it would seem, justified, for most are settled in the workers' favour.

Probably as a result of the arbitration legislation and their role in its operation, unions are dominantly involved in matters relating to pay and conditions of work. Unlike other countries, especially those with poorer social security legislation than New Zealand, the role as a welfare society is unimportant, almost unnecessary. Politically, the Federation of Labour tends to act as something of a 'conscience' for the country, over Vietnam, for example, and French nuclear testing. But, as in so many countries, union activity is generally in the hands of a few members, many with political aspirations of some sort: apathy is the order of the day. Within the union system, however, the older leaders are being outflanked by the growing militant stance of many white-collar groups and the formation of national unions, both of which give national prominence, in the news media, to their leaders.

FULL EMPLOYMENT

Most capitalist countries have a significant proportion of their workforce unemployed at any one time, many economic advisers to governments believing that to have a few per cent unemployed leads to a relatively stable economy. New Zealand, however, has consistently pursued a policy of full employment since it emerged from the depths of the 1930s depression when as many as 70,000 out of a workforce of 400,000 were either unable to find work or were on relief work. Considerable concern was expressed during a mild recession in 1969, for example, when there was an average of 5,000 unemployed, with a maximum of just over 9,000. (The latter figure represents less than one per cent of the national workforce.) It is believed that full employment brings stability, security, dignity and equality to society, and unemployment benefits are set to provide a basic income but not enough to encourage idleness—New Zealand is a 'welfare state', not a 'charity state'.

Full employment policies can bring several side-effects, however, especially when most sectors are suffering labour shortages.

They make it relatively easy for women to get work, both in large and small towns; clothing and textile firms often find it advantageous to open branch plants in the latter, where the labour force is relatively stable. But the policies also put the workers in strong bargaining positions, and employers have to offer wage increases and side-benefits in order to attract employees; such a situation is inflationary, especially given the 'ruling rates' system for adjusting the wages of government employees. High levels of labour turnover are also likely, especially in the larger places, and this can have marked effects on the costs of labour training. Immigration is frequently used to fill jobs, even unskilled tasks—for example, Fijians are sometimes brought in to act as scrub-cutters and Italians have been given temporary permits to work on several tunnelling projects. Firms may sponsor the immigration of skilled workers, who are bonded to them for two years, and receive government assistance in this, but other sections of the economy—such as house construction—may not be able to cope with a flood of new residents, so immigration is now closely controlled.

For the unemployed, benefits are available as a right—if the person is a *bona fide* New Zealand resident—once he or she has been out of work for seven days. The rates paid are the same as those for sickness and other benefits, and may be withdrawn if the recipient clearly refuses to work. Married women are, however, entitled to the benefit only if their husbands cannot support them, so that they often do not register and are under-represented in the unemployment figures; a wife's income may bring about a reduction in her husband's benefit. Occasionally, employment is provided in public works, and many men spent much time during the 1930s in very bleak conditions (perhaps under canvas) in such tasks as tree planting. Relief work is still provided when there are several thousand unemployed; local governments were given subsidies if they provided jobs in 1969.

WOMEN IN THE WORKFORCE

In rural societies, especially those in which a large proportion of the householders consists of self-employed agriculturalists, the role of married women—and of many children—is to assist with running the family holding. This was clearly the case in pioneer New Zealand, where many women played significant parts in the transformation of the landscape and the establishment of family farms. Farmers' wives are still expected to play their part in the rural economy—helping with the milking, perhaps, or feeding the members of the shearing gang. And, because farming is a seven-day-a-week, year-round occupation for most of their husbands, they are expected to be the major partner in the child-rearing venture.

These attitudes have persisted, despite urbanisation. There is still a large army of self-employed males, who expect considerable assistance from their wives, in the running of small shops and garages, for example. And the woman is still very much seen as a homemaker and childminder by most men (and many women); studies of child-rearing in New Zealand suggest a clear separation of roles in this, with the women very dominant. As a consequence, women are a small proportion of the paid labour force, in contrast with several other countries. Of 840,000 women aged 15–64, 334,000 reported an occupation other than housewife in 1971. About one-third of all married women are employed, though the percentage of married women in the female labour force has increased five-fold during the last decade.

Part of the problem of employment for women reflects the nature of the country's economy. There are few jobs available in rural areas and small towns, which is why many girls must go to the cities in their teens or early twenties, perhaps to become one of the 26,000 secretary/typists or 30,000 shopgirls. (Sixty per cent of employed women live in the four largest urban areas, compared with less than fifty per cent of employed males.) But there is obviously a deep social attitude against women, especially married women, working. More females than males, for example, have their school certificate (the first rung on the ladder of external examinations), but fewer climb to the next rungs in the schools, and whereas 42,000 New Zealand males aged over 15 have a university degree or diploma, they have only 17,000 female counterparts. And many jobs seem to be considered as male preserves—by many females as well as by the males themselves; in 1974 there were only three women professors in the universities, four women MPs (out of 87), and eleven women county councillors (out of 1,080).

The attitudes against female workforce participation are slowly changing. Equal pay was introduced for government servants in 1960, and an equal pay bill to cover all jobs was passed in 1972; its provisions will take effect in five stages, until full equality is attained in 1978. With the changing family structure already outlined, more married women are seeking work in their thirties and forties, whereas among younger generations there is a greater search for equality by members of both sexes. But still there is a strong current of feeling which believes in the separation of men's and women's roles, and women are occasionally used as 'status symbols', as in one party's campaign in recent local elections with its boast of three women candidates out of its total list of nineteen.

5

How They Move About

THE difficult topography, with its clothing of bush, has created many problems for the development of a transport system. The wide and shifting rivers, the steep and slip-prone hillsides, the cliffed coasts; all are major impediments to the construction of roads and railways. To move around the country, the Maori had a system of tracks but also made great use of canoes, for both coastal and inland movement; portages mark their land traverse from one inland waterway system to another. Coastal shipping predominated in the patterns of contact between the early pakeha settlements also, and development of a national internal transport system, whose capital assets are now worth almost a quarter of the country's fixed capital, has been a slow process towards the integration of the various parts of the two islands into a single economic unit.

ROAD AND RAIL

There are 94,000 kilometres of public roads in New Zealand, of which 9,600 are within the towns and cities. Less than half of this length is sealed; the majority of roads (virtually all of them outside the urban areas) are of loose metal or gravel. The provision of a sealed road is often unjustified in country areas because of the very low volumes of traffic carried, and in many places the likelihood of slips removing the road is a further reason for not going to the expense of sealing. Road construction is expensive in difficult country, costing up to $30,000 per kilometre. The liability to slipping in so many areas of friable, unprotected rock means that in wet weather a number of roads, including State Highways, may be blocked for several hours, or even washed away: isolated settlements can be cut off by road closures for several days after a storm. Maintenance costs are high, therefore. The total bill for roading is over $100 million annually (about two per cent of GNP), and for many county councils it is the major item of expenditure in their budget.

Oversight of the country's roading programme is the function of the National Roads Board which, through the Ministry of Works and Development, is entirely responsible for the 11,500 kilometres of State Highways. Half of the cost of roads in country areas is paid for by the NRB, and half by the local authorities; within urban areas the ratio is 1:2. To distribute the money the country is divided into twenty-two road districts among which finance is divided according to needs; NRB also makes decisions about its own programme of work within this framework. Large urban projects, such as motorways and traffic control systems, are financed through special grants and sanctioned loans.

Almost all of the NRB's income comes directly from the road users; three-quarters of income comprises the petrol tax of 21·4 cents per gallon. (At present, the country is moving to a metric system, and many petrol pumps now measure their flow in litres.) All vehicles must be licensed and covered for third-party risks; the licence fee and third-party insurance premium are collected together by the State, with the latter being transferred to an insurance company of the licensee's nomination. The fees/premiums are set at a sliding scale for cars (present cost, $25 for a 1,300cc vehicle), with separate sums for other vehicle types. Most vehicle owners also have a comprehensive insurance policy —with the company nominated for their third-party cover. One of the largest of the sixty-seven companies is the State Insurance Office; on a world scale, premiums are low.

New Zealand's roads are not fast; most main roads are two lanes wide. Until 1973—when a maximum speed of 50 miles per hour was introduced as a petrol conservation measure, later to be adopted as a permanent road safety measure in 1974—the maximum speed allowed on most roads was 55 mph, and 60 mph on a few better quality roads. There has been considerable upgrading of roads in recent years, however, and most of the

State Highways are now sealed over their entire length. So the ride is not uncomfortable, and what is lost in speed is more than made up, especially for the passenger, in the view through the window, whether the journey traverses the tidy farmlands of the plains, crosses the mountain ranges and basins, passes and gorges, or follows an attractive stretch of coast. The engineering feats of many of the roads, twisting up a steep incline, negotiating a wide river bed (there are very many bridges, some over a mile in length), or running parallel to a wave-battered beach, also add to the interest of many journeys.

The railway system was initiated by the provincial governments; most of it was developed by the central government and it is totally State owned. Its lines, both the trunk lines connecting the main cities and branches into the 'back country', have been major stimuli to settlement and the extension of farmland; the railway replaced the bullock cart and horse-drawn dray and very much widened the area from which produce could profitably be moved to the ports. Construction of lines has been very much impeded by topography, however, and completion of a national network was a long task. Many major engineering feats were performed from the first day. The Canterbury settlers, for example, began a tunnel through the walls of the extinct volcano separating Christchurch from its port of Lyttelton, only eleven years after their arrival in 1850; it was completed in 1867, ninety-seven years before a parallel road tunnel, 2 kilometres long, was opened.

Lines were built outwards from the main ports. A common gauge of 3ft 6in was soon established, its narrowness being more amenable to the sharp curves needed to negotiate the corrugated landscape. The first major connection was completed in 1879, with the relatively easy Christchurch–Dunedin–Invercargill line (590km), considerable lengths of which cross the flat plains of the South Island's east coast. Auckland and Wellington (682km) were not linked until 1908, the line necessitating the solution of many difficult engineering problems to cross the deeply dissected North Island hill country. One of the most spectacular pieces of engineering is the Raurimu Spiral, in the upper Wanganui River valley, where the line descends 120 metres. By the use of three horseshoes, two tunnels, and one complete loop, this descent was extended from 2 to 6·75 kilometres, and the grade reduced from 1 in 14 to 1 in 50. Christchurch was linked to Greymouth, Hokitika and Westport via the Otira tunnel (one of the three in the country over five miles long and the only one through the Southern Alps) in 1923. Inter-island rail movements have been possible only since the end of World War II. The line from Christchurch to Picton was completed in 1945, and a road-rail, roll-on/roll-off ferry service was introduced to Wellington from there in 1962. Two ferries now operate the service, together with two more designed for freight only. There is also a ferry link between Lyttelton and Wellington—one of its ships, the *Wahine*, was lost in a 1968 gale—whose future is presently very much in doubt.

Maintenance of the track is very expensive. Like the roads, the railways are prone to blockage and removal by slips, and all lines are liable to closure for a day or more. Derailments are common too, since ballasting is frequently very light. A considerable maintenance staff is retained, therefore. For a long time, many of these lived in small railway settlements along the track, but now are concentrated into a few centres. Branch lines, rural stations and sidings are also being closed, as the railways concentrate their efforts on inter-city movements; the present route length is about 4,000 kilometres. Steam engines were phased out by 1971, being replaced largely by diesel locomotives. (Some lines, notably the Wellington commuter lines, are electrified.)

The railway was the main link between farm and port for several decades, and also the main means of inter-city movement, but it has come under increasing competitive pressure from the improved road system. To protect the freight movement function, thereby reducing heavy road traffic volumes, regulations were introduced in the 1930s that goods may not be moved by road if a route is available that involves at least forty miles of rail and does not increase the total route length by more than a third. Some goods—notably livestock and perishable products—are exempt from this, and others are given a wider range. Since 1957, Blenheim and Nelson have been linked by a 'notional railway', a road service operated at railway rates and thus State-subsidised. Despite these measures, however, rail is losing the fight with road.

Passenger traffic on inter-city rail services has declined rapidly, in the face of competition from road and air transport. Slowness has always been a problem for the narrow-gauge trains; the Christchurch to Dunedin 'express' used to take nearly eight hours for the 340 kilometres, including several lengthy stops at which passengers purchased refreshments in the stations. (A staple diet of mugs of tea and hot meat pies was offered to the travellers.) Comfortable diesel expresses, with hostesses and refreshment cars, now operate the Christchurch–Dunedin–Invercargill, Wellington–Auckland (twice daily, one of them overnight), Wellington–Napier, and Wellington–New Plymouth services; other links are either by diesel railcar or in passenger wagons attached to freight services (such as the overnight 'cabbage train' from Picton to Christchurch). In addition, the Railways Department runs a quarter of the nation's inter-urban bus services, with a network of about 10,000 kilometres. Neither these nor the trains are patronised in large numbers, however, and the Railways Department's annual revenue from passengers amounts to only $2.44 for each New Zealander.

The road and rail networks are being upgraded to facilitate the movement of goods throughout the country, particularly to and from the ports. A detailed study commissioned by the government reported in 1974 that it would be economic to remove the forty-mile limit on rail-road competition, but this was before the implications of the rising oil prices were realised. Whether road, rail, or both are to be upgraded, much work is necessary. At present, several of the trunk railway lines in the North Island are operating at capacity because of the limitations on train length of the tight curves and steep grades (most lines are single-track, also); any efforts to expand capacity will require major engineering solutions to the problems posed by the terrain. The road system, on the other hand, is far from saturated, but a few articulated stock trucks, or even a car and caravan, can cause significant slowing of traffic movement on the narrow, winding sections, so that further use of this mode could create many traffic bottlenecks.

SEA AND AIR

The relative isolation of the various coastal settlements was a major reason for the provincial system of government adopted in pioneer pakeha New Zealand; it also produced a large number of small ports and a thriving coastal shipping system. By 1867 there were 112 ports dotted around the coast, at an average distance apart of only 97 kilometres. Of these, 26 handled overseas trade. A hierarchy of ports soon developed, however, with four major nodes—Otago (for Dunedin), Lyttelton (Christchurch), Wellington, and Auckland—dominating the international movements. From these, coastal vessels distributed imports around the two islands, returning with export cargoes for Britain.

As first the railways and then road transport developed, so the small ports declined, for coastal shipping was not as flexible as trains or trucks for delivering small consignments. Many of the ports, especially those at river mouths, are difficult to enter, even for small vessels, and the frequency of wrecks on harbour bars was undoubtedly a factor hastening port demise once alternative transport was available. Only thirty ports now operate. In overseas trade, most imports by value are handled by Whangarei, almost all of its trade being crude oil for the Marsden Point refinery, two-thirds of whose product is shipped elsewhere in New Zealand by coastal vessels. Tauranga's primacy in export volume reflects the movements of logs and newsprint through that port. Most other imports enter through either Auckland or Wellington. These two also handle a considerable volume of exports, but this aspect of overseas trade is more widely dispersed over the 'regional' ports. Timaru, Bluff and Napier handle much of the meat movements; Port Taranaki exports cheese; Napier, Lyttelton, Timaru and Otago move large tonnages of wool; Nelson is a major node for fruit movements. Nevertheless, four ships out of every ten entering New Zealand waters call first at Auckland, and three in every ten leave from there; ten other ports have more than a hundred vessels calling each year.

Coastal shipping is now used almost exclusively for the movement of bulk cargoes only, such as motor spirit from the Whangarei refinery, coal from Buller, and cement from the country's six works—three in each island. The railways dominate in the movement of long-distance general cargoes, with focus on the Cook Strait inter-island ferries. These latter are hard-pressed to cope, but efforts at sustaining other inter-island shipping services have met with little success.

Passenger movements of 200 kilometres or more, and especially those involving a crossing of Cook Strait, are dominated by the country's internal airline, the National Airways Corporation. The operations of this government corporation began after World War II, and it now has a fleet of twenty-five aircraft, including several Boeing 737s on its main route (Auckland–Wellington–Christchurch–Dunedin): the last Dakota was taken out of service in 1972. NAC now carries more than $1\frac{1}{2}$ million passengers annually on its flights serving twenty-six airports (an average of one flight for every two New Zealanders). The hub of its services is Wellington airport (Rongotai); 31,000 flights annually use its single runway which extends at one end into the turbulent waters of Cook Strait and at the other virtually to the edge of the more placid Wellington Harbour. Because of the windiness of Cook Strait, entry to and exit from this airport (which is only 5 kilometres from the city centre) is often bumpy. The other main airports are Auckland and Christchurch, each with more than fifty flights daily. One other airline runs a sizeable route network; Mt Cook Airways connects Christchurch and Dunedin to the alpine centres of Alexandra, Cromwell, Mt Cook, Milford Sound, and Queenstown, and also with Rotorua; in addition, seaplane services are operated in the Hauraki Gulf. Airlines have attempted to link small towns with the NAC net, but rarely succeeded in this enterprise for long.

Private flying is very popular, especially through the forty aero clubs with their average of five planes each. Over 100,000 hours are flown annually by club members. In all, over 3,000 New Zealanders have a pilot's licence (one to every thousand residents), and as many more are being trained.

Air freight is becoming increasingly important for the movement of small, valuable cargoes, as well as for much of the inter-island letter post. A service across Cook Strait was introduced by the New Zealand Air Force, on contract to the Railways Department; it is now run by Safeair (an NAC subsidiary). Air is the main means of contact with the Chatham Islands.

Widespread introduction of the 'big jets' produced a marked revolution in the mode of transport for international passengers to and from New Zealand. In the five years after 1967 the number of passengers arriving by liner almost halved; few ships now call—and many cargo liners no longer offer places for passengers. International air travel is very much focused on Auckland, which handles two-thirds of all movements. Just over 200,000 fly in annually, on routes connecting Auckland with the Far East, via Sydney, with London via Sydney or Los Angeles, and with many Pacific islands. Christchurch (140,000 passengers a year) and Wellington (80,000) have flights to both Sydney and Melbourne; Wellington has a link with Brisbane, also. New routes were opened in 1974 linking Christchurch and Wellington with Fiji, and Christchurch with Hong Kong, via Sydney.

Government control over airlines and airports is very close, and desirable. Programming of developments is relatively easy, therefore, although there has been some parochialism over whether Wellington as well as Christchurch should handle international flights. The internal airline, NAC, is in part run as a social service, with the main trunk route subsidising the costs of serving provincial towns.

With the port system, on the other hand, anarchy is much closer. The ports themselves are operated by locally-elected Harbour Boards, though these, as with other local governments, must obtain central permission to raise loans for capital works. There is a National Ports Authority which is to produce a national plan, but it has to counter both parochialism and the need for rapid decisions in a situation over which New Zealand has far from complete control. For example, it was decided, after several independent inquiries, that initially there would be only two ports to handle the New Zealand–Europe container traffic —Auckland and Wellington; after much had been invested in port facilities, the British Conference Lines decided not to develop a container service. At the same time, the South Island was clamouring for a container port, and various Harbour Boards were pushing their own case. Ports are expensive facilities; the employment and income they generate may be crucial to a town's economy: planning of the port system—in conjunction with plans for the feeder road and rail systems—is crucial for New Zealand's trading future.

COMMUTING

New Zealand is a land of car-owners; without their own vehicles, its inhabitants find it extremely difficult to move around their home town, let alone their home island. Four out of every five households have at least one motor-car, and one-quarter have two or more; in all there is one car to every three persons, plus one motor-cycle/scooter to every fifty. Of the workforce, forty-five per cent drive to their employment daily, and another ten per cent are carried as passengers.

Dependence on the motor-car for personal mobility is closely related to another feature of New Zealand, the very low housing densities of even the largest cities. Bus and train services for workers must cover long distances to attract sufficient custom, which makes them both expensive and infrequent; the scattered distribution of industrial employment around urban peripheries exacerbates the problem of providing financially-viable, public transport systems. (As it is, the railways are subsidised by the taxpayer and the buses by the ratepayer.) Rail services are important only in the dispersed Wellington urban area, where many employees are channelled into the harbourside city centre; almost 19,000 commuters use the trains there, compared with a daily 3,000 in Auckland, 500 in Christchurch and 900 in Dunedin. Bus and trolley services are provided by ten local authorities —and also by private companies and the Railways Department; with the exception of the service provided by Eastbourne Borough (a Wellington suburb), a loss is the usual summary of the annual accounts of these public undertakings.

There are few variations on the motorised journey-to-work. Christchurch, because of its flatness, is renowned among the larger cities for its high proportion of bicyclists, however. This mode of transport is popular with all sections of its society—the Anglican bishop is frequently seen cycling through the city streets—and 16,000 Christchurch workers, out of 110,000, regularly ride either a bicycle or motor-cycle to work. (Unfortunately, there is no available figure for cyclists alone: comparative figures for Auckland are 7,000 out of 267,000.) As the city roads have become almost saturated with cars, so cycling has become more hazardous and there are many fewer cyclists on the streets today than a decade ago.

Major traffic problems have been caused by the proliferation of car ownership and use. Most towns have their bottlenecks— often level crossings since bridges are uncommon and the railway usually passes close to, if not through, a town's centre. In the largest cities, drastic surgery to the road system is proving necessary to facilitate car movement. Auckland already has several miles of urban motorway, bringing traffic into the city centre from both approaches to its isthmus location. On the north side, the motorway uses the Auckland Harbour Bridge. Carrying a four-lane highway, this was opened in 1959, and such was the residential development it generated on the North Shore— formerly reached by ferry only—that within five years it was saturated during the very peaked rush-hour (4.30 pm–5.30 pm) which characterises New Zealand. Four extra lanes were added outside the main arch—the 'Nippon clip-on' as it is known—and 19,000,000 vehicles now use the bridge each year: another bridge is being planned. Wellington, too, has motorways focused on its centre—that to the Hutt Valley follows a major fault line —and a system is being developed in Christchurch, though there political fighting and conservationist activity is causing continued debate and re-thinking.

Motorists pay an initially high price for the privilege of using the roads. All cars are either imported complete or assembled from largely imported parts. High transport costs from Britain, Japan and even Australia, added to high duties, mean that, for example, a British car may cost half as much again as in its home market. For many years, purchase of a new car was difficult. To control the outflow of overseas exchange a deposit of money held overseas was necessary (part of this was remitted to the New Zealand government), and money could not be remitted overseas for this purpose. Hence second-hand cars held their value and, because only a few people could obtain a new car, at a list price, the late model, second-hand car was often valued higher than a new one. The 'no remittance' scheme no longer operates, but in the full-employment, inflationary economy since it was removed, supply of cars has been unable to meet demand and second-hand values remain high. Further, cars tend to remain on the roads longer. There are no hazards—such as salt to melt snow, which is unheard of in all except Dunedin of the main cities—to enhance decay, and local initiative tends to keep cars running much longer than they might elsewhere. To ensure road safety, all vehicles must obtain a warrant of fitness every six months, and no car can be sold without a warrant issued in the preceding month. So the high initial investment is often repaid, and running costs are relatively cheap—notably registration and insurance but also petrol, of which there are only two grades, super costing 16 cents per litre. Recent changes in sales tax have been designed to encourage purchase of small cars.

6

How They Learn

PROVISION of education opportunities and facilities is perhaps one of the most apparent aspects of New Zealand's egalitarianism. School attendance is compulsory for all between the ages of six and fifteen, inclusive; most children start at school on their fifth birthday. Basic costs are met by the State, but, even during the compulsory years, education is not completely free. As with so many aspects of the country's life, the education system—particularly beyond the pre-school years—is highly centralised, with most of the major decisions being taken by the Department of Education in Wellington. The present, however, is a period of marked experiment and change.

PRE-SCHOOL AND PLAY CENTRE

Researchers in many countries have been indicating the great educational and social values of schooling for children aged between three and five, with the result that priority is being placed on provision of the needed facilities. In New Zealand, two parallel institutions provide these.

The Free Kindergarten Association runs over 300 kindergartens nationwide. Although an independent body, the association receives much of its finance from the government. Its teachers are paid by the State after training in a special Department of Education college; a State bursary is received during the training period. Government makes a two-thirds grant for the purchase of land and of basic equipment, and for construction of the kindergarten buildings. A loan will be provided also, to cover the remaining costs; alternatively, the government will give a subsidy of $2 for every dollar raised towards the cost of the kindergarten by the local community.

The Play Centre Association is supported to a lesser extent by public money, and each play centre itself is a relatively independent organisation. Small initial grants and contributions to maintenance costs are received from the public purse, but the centres rely on parental support and involvement for both finance and labour. Supervisors are trained by the association, and paid by the centre they work at; a parent of each child attending a centre must attend a set number of sessions each term to assist the supervisors. There is a small attendance fee; parents are active in raising money for the development and operation of their centre, and are expected to assist at the regular 'working bees', when most construction and maintenance is undertaken.

Kindergartens and play centres are not full-time institutions (most children would attend for only two, three or four half-days each week), though many operate two 'shifts'. They are certainly not child-minding centres; in aims they vary slightly, with play centres requiring parental involvement and placing all of their emphasis on 'structured play' whereas kindergartens are more of a bridge in their activities between home and school. The existence of both types depends on local action and interest; the financial provisions reflect State benevolence rather than State socialism. In many areas it is difficult to obtain a place for a child, so that attendance from the third to fifth birthdays is more theoretical than real. At present some 41,000 attend, approximately one-third of all children in the relevant age-group. Of these, 17,000 attend one of the 600 play centres, which are generally much smaller than kindergartens. The play centre movement is the more popular among Maori, particularly rural Maori groups.

PRIMARY, INTERMEDIATE, AND SECONDARY

Primary schools cater for the five to eleven year olds. One-tenth of these children, about 50,000, attend one of the 300 private schools; ninety per cent of these are at Roman Catholic institutions. In both State and private schools, the ratio of pupils to teachers is 28:1 (it is nearer 20:1 in the non-Roman Catholic private schools), and over half of the children are in classes of less than thirty-five. The ratio of male to female teachers is 6:10.

All State primary schools operate a standard syllabus, comprising reading and writing, mathematics, social studies, arts and crafts, science, physical and health education, and music. The same basic materials are used throughout the country: a child's reading level, for example, is assessed by the book presently being read, out of a set sequence, this being beneficial for students transferring between schools. Text books are provided free, but parents must purchase all required expendable materials. The State provides only a basic set of buildings and equipment; extras such as halls, libraries, playground equipment, and swimming pools (common to most schools) must be financed by the local community. There is thus considerable parental involvement, in money-raising activities and the almost universal 'working bees'; the result may be considerable inter-school variation in provision of facilities.

Administration of the primary schools is highly centralised. Most decisions are made by the district office (there are ten of these) of the Department of Education. The relevant body is the Education Board, among whose functions is the allotment of all new teachers, during their first two years after training, rather than a system of advertisement, application, and selection. Within each school, the head has considerable powers, though departmental grading determines how many teachers at each level in the career hierarchy can be employed there. A School Committee, elected by the parental community at a public meeting, oversees the school's operation. There will probably be a number of other support groups, such as a Home and School Association whose main function is usually money-raising.

Until the Second World War, there was a large number of small primary schools, notably in rural areas, where one- and two-teacher establishments were very common. There has been a marked increase in average school size since then, partly because of the growing concentration of population into urban areas, and partly because of rural school consolidation policies.

About one-tenth of the 2,000 primary schools presently open have fewer than twenty-five pupils, and a half have less than 110; at the other extreme, one-tenth have more than 500. Rural school consolidation has allowed more appointment of specialist teachers to country areas, but it also means that some pupils have to travel considerable distances each day. Where it is possible—which is rare—public transport is used. In many areas, contract buses are provided, often by a garage proprietor as a supplementary source of income. In smaller settlements, the Department of Education provides a bus: it will be driven by one of the teachers, and a small school bus parked beside the school house is a not infrequent sight. A consequence of the dispersed rural settlement pattern, and the long journeys (in some cases an hour or more), is the relatively short school day, typically ending at 3 pm or 3.30 pm.

Progress through the State school system involves three sequences, organised largely by age. The first two years, the infant classes—or 'primers' as they are commonly known—cater for the five and six year olds; the next four—the 'standards'—are for those aged seven to eleven; the last sequence, extending to the school-leaving age, is termed the 'forms'. Primary schools provide for the 'primers' and 'standards': the two groups are usually separated within the school, with the former under the control of a senior infant teacher and the latter under the head teacher and his or her deputy.

After primary school, about half of all State pupils proceed to an intermediate school, which is akin to the American junior high school and the British middle school. The intermediate school provides a bridge between primary and secondary school for Form 1 and 2 students, offering a wider range of practical subjects than the former and also more specialised teaching. If such schools are available, parents have no choice as to which school their children attend, while for primary schools choice is allowed. Where there is no intermediate, pupils will probably obtain their Form 1 and 2 education at the primary school; most of the exceptions to this occur in rural areas where, to obtain an adequate total enrolment, Forms 1 and 2 may be included in the high schools.

Secondary schools—known as high schools—provide the final

years of education for all pupils. Just under a fifth stay for only two years (Forms 3 and 4); a further third stay an extra year; about a quarter proceed to Form 6 and a fifth to Form 7. Some 220 State high schools cater for about 150,000 pupils, employing 9,000 teachers (sixty per cent of them male). About three-quarters of the pupils are at coeducational establishments. Single-sex schools—there are twenty-five each for boys and girls —are commonly the older foundations in the larger cities, and are no longer being built. All of the schools are comprehensive, in that there is no selective entrance test, and, increasingly, their catchment areas are zoned giving parents and pupils little, if any, choice. Many are large establishments—up to 2,000 pupils on the one site. They are streamed—academic, general and vocational strands are common, and researchers have shown that this leads to the same sort of channelling and status-ascribing which characterises systems such as the grammar school/modern school dichotomy that still operates in parts of Britain.

Some rural areas produce insufficient pupils to support a full high school, and for such districts variants of the basic system have been designed. Most common is the District High School, which combines primary, intermediate and secondary departments; sixty of these schools cater for 4,000 pupils. As an alternative, secondary and intermediate departments are combined to establish a Form 1–7 High School. The role of both types of school is diminishing, however, and consolidation programmes are establishing full high schools for many large rural areas.

Pupils living in very remote areas—such as lighthouses or high country sheep stations—may have no school accessible to them. To cater for these, and for others who for reasons such as illness may be unable to attend school regularly, there is a Wellington-based correspondence school, which broadcasts daily over the national radio network. Its 160 teachers and 26 tutors provide courses for about 7,000 pupils; 1,100 of these are full-time primary students and a further 500 are full-time secondary, with the remainder taking correspondence lessons part-time. The smaller number of secondary pupils reflects the common trend in remote areas of sending these children to boarding establishments in the towns and cities. There are thirty-seven State secondary schools which take boarders, and more than 2,000 pupils are given bursaries to support them at such establishments. (Similar bursaries are given to 1,500 pupils whose parents choose to board them at private secondary schools.)

Administration of secondary schools is more devolved than that of their primary counterparts. Each has a Board of Governors, comprising representatives of various groups, such as the Department of Education, the university in whose district the school lies, the former pupils, and, in a few cases, present pupils. Probably the Board's most important role is in the appointment of a head teacher—from a short-list of applicants drawn up by the Department. In its other tasks, of administering the government grant and appointing staff, it usually relies heavily on the head, who thus has much independence of action, if not autonomy.

Outside the State system there are 115 private secondary schools, with about 30,000 students and 1,500 teachers. Most of these schools are religious foundations—Roman Catholic schools are most common—and virtually all are single-sex. Few are 'public' schools in the British tradition but of these the most typical is Christ's College, in Christchurch, at which the boater is still worn. In the non-Catholic schools, in particular, there is an amalgam of local fee-payers, who live at home, and boarders; since many of the latter come from the 'richer' farming families, the private secondary schools are clustered in centres of sheep-farming districts, such as Christchurch, Masterton, and Napier-Hastings.

The question of State aid to private schools has occasioned much debate in recent years, both politically (with parties vying for the Catholic vote) and led by unions of teachers in the State system (which are, not surprisingly, against all aid). Presently, there are grants made for the purchase of certain items of equipment, such as science laboratories, and towards teachers' salaries; if schools meet the requirements of the Department of Education's inspectors, they receive free text books on the same basis as State schools.

'Old-boy networks', typical of the British 'public' schools, are also products of New Zealand's 'private' schools, though they are by no means as influential in determining the course of the nation's affairs, or the success of various individuals in their conduct. Somewhat similar networks—though they are almost entirely social and sporting in function—characterise many of the older State high schools, especially the single-sex establishments.

The course content of secondary schools, as with primary schools, is closely prescribed and overseen by the Department of Education. Forms 1–4 have a common core syllabus, comprising English, social studies, general science, mathematics, music, arts and crafts, and physical education. From Form 5 on, students specialise; their courses are very much constrained by, and oriented to, the sequence of external examinations. The first of these—taken at the end of Form 5—is School Certificate, in which passes are granted for individual subjects. A candidate must offer English, history or geography or a language, and either mathematics or science among his/her subjects. University Entrance, which is the basic qualification for admittance to that institution, is taken at the end of Form 6. Most schools have the right to accredit pupils with this qualification through internal assessment. (School Certificate is a series of externally-marked examinations.) Accreditation is closely scrutinised to avoid injustices; pupils not accredited, and those whose schools do not have the right to accredit, may sit an externally-assessed examination set by the Universities Entrance Board. Successful University Entrance candidates may proceed directly to university, but most now remain at school for the Form 7 year, at the end of which they take either the Bursaries examination, or that plus the Scholarships examination. These, too, are set and marked by the Universities Entrance Board, and are the basis for financial awards to support university study.

Of the school-leavers in 1970, forty-three per cent had achieved no formal qualification. One-quarter passed one or more subjects at School Certificate, one-eighth at University Entrance, and one-seventeenth at either Bursaries or Scholarship. The remainder obtained one or two recently introduced qualifications aimed mainly at students not intending a tertiary education—the Sixth Form Certificate and the Higher School Certificate.

New Zealand's schools have been criticised frequently for their uniformity and authoritarianism. School uniforms are generally compulsory. For boys, they are usually drab, comprising grey socks, shirts, shorts, and sweaters (no jackets, although grey suits are common at private high schools); girls usually wear blouses and skirts in winter, checked cotton dresses in summer. Greater freedom is presently being introduced, however, with, for example, less fuss about the boys' hair length and permission for girls to wear trousers.

The authoritarian rule, with an emphasis on strict discipline, is now being relaxed, with senior pupils in particular being allowed greater freedom. Within the classroom, although there has always been much learning through discovery ('project work'), there is a widely held belief that there is too much 'spoon feeding', especially in preparation for the external examinations. Curricula are being made more flexible, in part a consequence of the action of teachers through their unions. And teachers' careers prospects are, since 1974, no longer tied to the grading which they receive as the result of a regular visit from the Department of Education's inspectors.

TERTIARY EDUCATION

Universities were established in three of the four main cities within a few decades of their settlement. Two—the Universities of Otago and Canterbury—have already celebrated centennials and the third—Auckland—will soon follow them; a university at the fourth city—Victoria University of Wellington—was not inaugurated until 1897. Until the last decade, these four institutions were constituent colleges of the University of New Zealand. They became separate entities in 1962, under the overall control of the Universities Grants Committee. This acts as an intermediary between universities and government; it distributes research moneys and the quinquennial grant, acts on building proposals, and, through its Curriculum Committee, oversees course developments. The separate Universities Entrance Board maintains common entrance standards through the Entrance, Bursaries, and Scholarships examinations.

Universities were created at the two largest cities below the 'four main centres' during the 1960s. The University of Waikato at Hamilton began as a branch college of the University of Auckland; at Palmerston North, a former branch of Victoria University was amalgamated with an agricultural college to form the Massey University of the Manawatu. These universities now have 1,000 and 2,700 students respectively: numbers at the older four are Auckland, 9,300; Victoria, 5,800; Canterbury, 6,800 (plus 1,000 at its constituent agricultural college at Lincoln); and Otago, 5,200. During the late 1960s, student numbers increased rapidly, and a seventh university was planned to open in 1976 in a northern suburb of Auckland. Growth is now negligible, however, and the plans have been put into abeyance.

The entrance qualification to all universities is success at the University Entrance examination; for persons aged over 21, the matriculation requirement is School Certificate or an equivalent. The 'open door' is fairly wide, therefore, and about eleven per cent of the eligible age group enter through it each year. Most students get some State financial support. A fees bursary is available to all who are successful in their courses; *bona fide* full-time students may obtain fees and allowances bursaries, which cover tuition costs and provide an allowance, which increases annually over a possible total of six years' study. Supplementary grants are made to successful candidates at the Bursaries and Scholarships examinations. Other sources of finance are available from government departments, usually as attractive bursaries offered in return for a bond to work for the relevant department for a given number of years after graduation.

Students are strongly encouraged through the grants sytem to attend the university in their home town, if there is one. Boarding allowances are paid only to those who must live away from home, which for those normally resident in a university town means that they must be enrolled in courses not provided at their 'home' institution. As a consequence, some forty per cent of students live at home.

The first degree undertaken by most New Zealand students— in arts, science, or commerce—is the bachelor's, which is based on the liberal traditions of the Scottish system. This may involve the student in courses from at least five separate disciplines. After it, a variety of honours degrees is offered, some taking one and others two years. In addition, each of the four older universities has its special schools, providing vocational and professional training within closely determined criteria. All four offer law and accountancy, for example; Auckland and Canterbury teach engineering, Auckland and Otago medicine, and Canterbury (Lincoln) and Massey have large agricultural faculties. Finally, Massey University offers a wide range of its courses to about 2,000 external students, by correspondence and occasional residential schools.

Progress through the university, particularly its general degrees, is frequently slow, and there are many failures en route. Only about half of the students presently graduating finish their course in the minimum time (three years for a bachelor's degree); another quarter will have taken one extra year. Drop-out and exclusion (for total failure) rates are substantial and, as a consequence of political pressure, the universities are becoming much tougher in administering exclusion policies. Part-time students are common; 9,000 in 1970 out of a total of 32,000. Many of these are government employees (including teachers and trainee teachers); some intend to complete a degree—and perhaps commence or recommence full-time study—but many are taking only isolated units of the total degree, perhaps for interest or to further career prospects. There are also 2,400 overseas students (one in twelve of the total); Malaysians form the largest contingent, and Auckland and Canterbury—because of their engineering schools—are the most popular institutions for them. Three-quarters of the overseas students are privately financed, with the New Zealand government supporting two-thirds of the remainder, mostly through the Colombo Plan.

Until the 1960s, teaching dominated university staff time, and there were many evening classes for part-timers. Graduate students seeking a doctorate usually went to Britain or North America. The research function is now given much greater priority and staff teaching loads are much lighter; most postgraduates stay at home. Isolation within the international academic community is a problem for researchers, but staff are encouraged, by generous grants on top of salary, to take regular periods of overseas leave. In the past, many lecturers and professors were recruited abroad, notably in Britain, but there is an increasing proportion of local products on the teaching staffs.

Administration is largely by departments for individual disciplines, in which appointed heads hold considerable power.

Whereas the universities have considerable autonomy, the teachers' training colleges are directly controlled by the Department of Education. There are nine of these colleges—at least one in each of the six university cities—catering for about 7,500 students annually. They offer a variety of courses, though not at every college; secondary teachers, for example, are trained at Auckland and Christchurch only. Courses are of two main types, the one-year programme for university graduates and the three-year for full-time teacher trainees. (The latter may also be part-time students at either universities or technical institutes.) Studentships, which bond the recipient to work for the Department—at a school determined by the Department in the case of primary teachers—are paid on a sliding scale by year of study. Some 2,000 full-time university students are among the bonded group at present, which requires liaison between colleges and universities—some universities allow the college staffs to teach introductory courses for them—and makes university arts faculties, in particular, aware of their students' vocations and needs.

The third arm of the tertiary education system, the technical institutes, is by far its weakest. Until 1945, technical education was provided at specified technical high schools, at the secondary level. There are now eleven institutes, offering a very wide range of courses to 100,000 or more apprentices and others each year, and there is also a Technical Correspondence Institute, in contact with more than 15,000 students. Unfortunately most of the institutes operate in very unfavourable conditions, with poor staff/student ratios and buildings scattered over a wide area. (One institute was recently having to teach a group in a barn, several miles from its city-centre campus.) To correct these problems, the institutes are presently receiving high priority in the allocation of expenditure. Between 1951 and 1971 their spending increased by twenty-one per cent annually, compared with twelve per cent for education as a whole, but they still receive only four per cent of the total education budget, about half of the expenditure on teacher training and a quarter of that on universities.

EDUCATION AND SOCIETY

New Zealanders do not rate education as an end in itself as is the case in some Celtic countries, but nor do they consider it merely as a commodity to be purchased. Its relevance to national social and economic development is widely recognised, as reflected in increased government expenditure. Spending on buildings increased tenfold—to $50.4 million—in the twenty years to 1971, and current expenditure increased eleven times to $287.4 million. As a consequence, educational spending has doubled as a percentage of the government budget, being fifteen per cent at present. But, in comparison with West European countries, New Zealand's expenditure of just over six per cent of its national income on education is relatively small.

Although politicians and public alike generally accept the need for a large educational budget, there is considerable debate over the best division of the expenditure. Rapid university expansion, especially in arts and social sciences, during the 1960s has raised many eyebrows; a need is advanced for expenditure more 'relevant' to the country's needs, both within the universities (emphasising agricultural, biological and related research, for example) and without, as into the technical institutes. Indeed, there is much debate at all educational levels, and during 1973–4 there was a nationwide Educational Development Conference, which involved both large public seminars—many addressed by invited overseas experts—and innumerable neighbourhood discussion groups 'tapping the grass roots'. (The Development Conference is a common New Zealand device for eliciting planning priorities; several were held in the 1960s, culminating in the 1968 National Development Conference.) The Minister of Education wanted the conference to tap public opinion, with the intention of legislation by early 1975 following collation of all the seminar and discussion group reports. Whether this conference indeed 'tapped' all of the grass roots or was rather structured to favour certain, more articulate sectors of the community, the rate of innovation in the educational system has already speeded up. One Christchurch high school, for example, sends many of its pupils out for industrial experience on one day a week. And independent outfits have emerged, such as the Learning Exchange which puts people wishing instruction in a particular topic in touch with a teacher.

Continuing education for adults is another indicator of the generally favourable New Zealand attitude to education. Organisations such as the Workers' Educational Association have a long history of wide activity, and the Extension Departments of the various universities offer a wide range of courses. Both are increasingly having to face the competition of television. Evening courses in arts and crafts are offered at most high schools, plus a range of lecture series in current affairs and academic subjects, and there are currently plans to co-ordinate these and other adult educational activities at community colleges; the first was opened in Hawke's Bay in 1975. Continuing education for teachers is also vigorously pursued by the Department of Education, which runs several residential 'houses' for in-service courses.

In general, New Zealand's education system probably caters very well for the average student, at every stage. It is perhaps not particularly well structured to meet the needs of those at either extreme of the ability continuum, producing numerous frustrations and leading, for example, to a continuing 'brain drain' of those who find too little support for their innovativeness within a small and fairly conservative educational establishment.

7

How They Amuse Themselves

*Down under, they're
Mad over, their
Rugby, racing, and beer.*

NEW ZEALAND has a reputation in many parts of the world as a sporting nation. Its best-known representatives are probably the 'All Blacks', the national rugby union fifteen, and, increasingly, the national cricket eleven. Elsewhere, its rowing crews, such as the eight which won a gold medal at the 1972 Munich Olympics, or its racehorses may be better known. Many individual sportsmen are world famous also, such as athletes Murray Halberg and Peter Snell of the early 1960s, Dick Tayler, Dick Quax, John Walker and Rod Dixon of the early 1970s. And New Zealand has provided world leaders in motor racing (Bruce Maclaren and Denny Hulme), speedway (Ronnie Moore, Barry Briggs, and Ivan Mauger have between them won the world championship ten times), golf (Bob Charles has long been the world's leading left-hander), and mountaineering (Ed Hillary was one of the first two to climb Everest), to mention but a few. Many countries produce renowned international sportsmen, of course, but few, particularly when population size is taken into account, produce either the depth of talent or the number of participants as New Zealand. Active sport dominates non-working life there to a greater extent than in most other countries, and sporting activities are very much major users of leisure and recreation time.

THE OUTDOOR SOCIETY

The year-round temperate climate in most parts of the country encourages outdoor activity in all seasons. There is a clear national ethos that emphasises the benefits of participation in team sports, which is probably part of the egalitarian tradition, although the stress is very much on male sports and recreational activities. A consequence of this is that there is virtually no professionalism in sport, except for a few administrators. New Zealand is a nation of players, not of spectators. Large crowds are drawn to the major stadia for some interprovincial rugby games, as well as for all international rugby and cricket tests, but few other contests draw many onlookers. Supporters' clubs and the other paraphernalia of professional sport in Europe and North America are weak, if indeed they exist, though there is a wide following for most teams and individuals through press, radio and TV; New Zealand is certainly a country of amateur 'experts', many of whom will stay up into the early hours of the morning to listen to or watch a broadcast of a match being played in Europe or South Africa.

Sporting activity extends beyond participation in team and individual games to a more general ethos that emphasises physical fitness, as a form of *machismo*. Jogging—running through the streets or round a park—is undertaken by a large section of the male population, of all ages and walks of life. Indeed it is virtually impossible to drive around a New Zealand town or city, at any hour of the day or night, without coming across individual or group joggers, some of them active sportsmen keeping fit, some running simply for health reasons, and a few, it would seem, for the social bond. Among women, yoga groups are increasingly popular.

But this intense sporting activity is only a part of New Zealand's outdoor culture. One activity in which a majority, and certainly a majority of married persons, frequently participate is gardening. Indeed, it is often argued that many New Zealanders work much harder at this leisure activity during their two-day weekend than they do at their five-day jobs. (There is little evening activity as night falls rapidly, even in mid-summer, and there has been no daylight-saving adjustment of clocks.) Flowers, trees, shrubs, vegetables and of course weeds, all grow so easily and rapidly that it is a waste of land not to tend a garden carefully, although younger and older generations seem at present to have less interest than has gone before, as indicated by the trend to higher-density living. Not only is the garden used as a source of fresh foods and flowers, however; a casual drive through most settlements will indicate the intense pride many have in the appearance of their plots—especially the street frontages—and the great amount of time invested in them. Many places run competitions both for individual gardens (for factories as well as for homes) and for 'best-kept streets'; the latter occasionally produce intense social pressure on a recalcitrant gardener in a street where the majority are keyed up to win. Individual households are often very much over-capitalised in the equipment they possess for gardening; nearly two-thirds of all households own a motor mower, for example, for the weekly or twice-weekly (in summer) task. (In some areas, lawns must be mown throughout the year.)

Beyond the immediate home are two areas which many New Zealanders visit both frequently and regularly—the beach and the bush. The coastal waters, especially those of the South Island, are generally rather cold, but this does not deter large numbers of swimmers and surfboard riders, especially in the late December–January holiday season. Many beaches are dangerous, with strong rip currents and occasional visits by sharks; near to towns and cities, the most popular are patrolled by volunteer groups and safe areas for swimming are delimited, but deaths from drowning are still common. Surf life-saving is, in fact, a major summer 'sport'; it has something military about it—because of the discipline needed when saving lives in the sea—and there is a whole hierarchy of carnivals and contests leading up to the national championships in late February. In general, except in or close to a large city, beaches are rarely, if ever, crowded; it is very easy to get a large stretch almost to oneself, except for the almost ubiquitous sandflies wherever beach and bush are in close proximity.

Boating, in both coastal and inland waters, is another very

popular aquatic pastime and sport. About 80,000 households (one in every ten) have a boat of some kind—dinghy or yacht, cabin cruiser or jetboat—which may be used in racing or merely for 'messing about on the river'. Water-skiing is a popular sport with motor boats. Many of the vessels are kept conspicuously at home, in backyard or garage, and are towed to the beach every time they are to be used.

Finally, and not surprisingly, New Zealand is a nation of swimmers. There is some element of a sport in this—as was emphasised at the 1974 Commonwealth Games in Christchurch —but there are few competitive pools; most swim for relaxation. As already noted, small pools are very common at primary schools, and these are frequently open to the public at weekends and holidays, especially in country districts. Lidos are commonly provided by local governments in towns and cities and an increasing number of households have their own small back garden pool.

A wide range of pursuits is undertaken in the 'bush'—gentle walks, long tramps, deer shooting, mountaineering, and skiing, for example—and an increasing proportion of New Zealanders is participating in these. Walks of varying length and difficulty are laid out in National and Forest Parks, and also in Scenic Reserves; they often fulfil an educational purpose, with pamphlets and signs describing the local flora. There are many longer tracks for tramps of a day or more in duration, and on some of these tramping clubs maintain huts for overnight stays. Some tracks are very popular—such as the Heaphy Track in the north-west of the South Island which is presently a source of controversy because of a proposed road through the area. A few, such as the Milford Track in Fiordland and the Routeburn Track from Lake Wakatipu, are used by organised parties.

Many peoples' bush activities do not take them far from the main roads. Those who penetrate deeper into the bush—which is rarely far away—usually do so on an organised basis, for the potential dangers are great, not only of climbing accidents and of shooting mishaps for hunters, but also of simply getting lost, especially when the weather closes in. There is a very efficient search and rescue organisation, involving National Park rangers, police, and the air force, which is frequently called into action, but deaths in the back country are still far from unusual.

In the more remote bush, deerstalking is a popular activity, and the Deerstalkers' Club lobby is a strong one on a range of issues involving the high country. Deer, chamois, and thar, and also wild pigs, can be found in considerable numbers in many areas, but the individual stalker is often in competition with the professional hunter, who stalks by helicopter and sells his venison in the United States. Companies hunting in National Parks must be licensed, and they are fiercely competitive in their search for game.

Many bush and farming pursuits take on a sporting side at certain times of the year. Wood-chopping competitions are usual at agricultural and pastoral shows; shearing contests culminate in the national Golden Shears award; ploughing competitions and sheep-dog trials both have their supporters. For many townspeople, however, the main contact with the countryside is at an annual picnic, of sports club or church, Sunday school or trade union, works social group or PTA. Autumn weekends are the times for most of these; bush or coastal reserves with barbecue facilities are the common venues. The large number of them is occasionally realised by the casual visitor to such a place, or when the local radio gives a list of cancellations on a wet Sunday morning.

SPORT

Rugby union football is New Zealand's national game, and the dominant winter sport. It is organised through the national Rugby Football Union and a series of provincial and subprovincial unions. Boys are initiated to its rigours and competitive nature by the age of seven. Although it is played at schools, most boys play their rugby—and all other sports—for a club side, practising one night a week (often under floodlights) and playing on Saturday morning or afternoon. The season lasts from April till September.

The lower competitive grades are organised by age and weight; in Christchurch, for example, the lowest is the 'Under 5 stones, under 7s', and there is a ritual weighing-in and inspection of birth certificates at the season's start. Higher grades are organised by ability. All teams play in competitive leagues; many grades have several divisions. A large proportion of the young male population plays—over 6,000 in Christchurch, for example—and the playing fields are a mosaic of brightly coloured shirts from 9 am on Saturday till about 4 pm. There is also a large population of 'assistants', including trained referees who officiate at all games. Each team has at least one coach, so allowing a large number of ex-players to continue an association with the game. And, especially in the boys' grades, there is often a substantial number of vocal parents on the sidelines, perhaps getting more from the games than their young children, who are being introduced to a sport in which the intricate rules and need for teamwork are initially hard to grasp.

At provincial level, there is no league or knock-out competition. Each province has a standard set of fixtures with its neighbours. Every second year or so it probably tours the other island, playing several provinces; in return, such provinces visit it on a quasi-regular basis. Plenty is at stake in these 'friendly' games, however, including both the prestige of the province and the chance for the individual to advance his claims for the coveted 'All Black' jersey. The highpoint of inter-provincial rugby is the Ranfurly Shield, which is held by a team until defeated in a challenge game, held almost invariably at the holder's home ground. The holder decides which challenges to accept each year, balancing the temptation to play only weak unions, and thereby retain the Shield and boost gate receipts, against the knowledge that if it refuses too many challenges it will find it hard to obtain one once the Shield is lost. Frequently the Shield is held by one province for a season or two (playing perhaps six to eight challenges in each); it may then change hands several times in rapid succession until a strong province gains possession.

New Zealand's international prowess at rugby was established early in the century by two highly successful tours of the British Isles. (On one, in 1905, the only defeat resulted from a still-debated controversial try scored by Wales.) Many All Blacks tend to become almost folk-heroes; the press frequently announces the death of a star of forty years ago, whose exploits are probably recalled by only a few, since in those days of infrequent tours, most players appeared in few games. The status of the All Blacks slipped after test defeats in South Africa in 1970, against the British Isles at home in 1971, in several games in Britain and France in 1972–3, and against England at Auckland in 1973, but 1974 saw renewed success on a tour of Great Britain. The game is probably as popular as ever among the armchair critics and selectors, but indications are that the depth of talent is not as great as it was. It is probably an over-organised sport, at every level, giving many men a 'little bit of power'.

The Rugby League code (13-a-side) is strong only in Auckland, Wellington, Westland, and Christchurch. Occasionally, the international side performs well, but then loses its best players to the riches of the professional clubs in Sydney. In Christchurch over 2,000 play every Saturday.

Association football (soccer) has made rapid advances in popularity during the last decade. Television has made a major contribution to this. The New Zealand Rugby Football Union is a very conservative body, and only since 1973 has it allowed any live coverage of games, its policy being designed to protect local clubs against a growth of armchair supporters. Soccer has been widely televised, however (as has Rugby League). Initially this involved the showing of films of British professional games, introducing viewers to the skills and emotions in a period of English international supremacy. In 1969 a National League was formed in New Zealand, and half of one of these games is shown live on most Saturdays. At present many of the players in this league have been imported from Britain, but there is growing grass-roots support, and in Christchurch now over 4,000 play each week. The boys' grades are very strong, perhaps reflecting the easier rules and principles for young persons. Soccer authorities, too, are very eager to promote their sport in the schools, while the rugby unions are very much establishment-oriented, which makes it difficult for new schools to penetrate the established circuit of fixtures.

For women, opportunities for outdoor winter sports are few, and the activities are rarely given much publicity. Most common is netball—until recently called outdoor basketball—which has 3,000 players in Christchurch each Saturday. Hockey (in which

New Zealand is strong internationally) is played by both sexes, but is dominantly a male sport.

Participation in organised team games is much lower during the summer, no doubt because of the counter-attractions of beach, bush, and garden. Cricket is the most widely publicised game; it is enjoying high prestige at present after near-victories over England, in England, during 1973 and a defeat of Australia at Christchurch in 1974. As with rugby, the sport is organised into competitive leagues and some 2,000 turn out each Saturday afternoon in Christchurch. Most grounds are in public parks, with overlapping outfields, so that spectators can enjoy several games at the one time. The national competition is a league of six sides (Auckland, Wellington, Canterbury, Otago and Northern and Central Districts) which play each other in three-day matches during December–January to determine possession of the Plunket Shield. The Hawke Shield is competed for on a challenge basis by sub-provincial sides, and there is now a series of one-day Sunday matches. Touring teams usually visit in March, after a series in Australia.

Although cricket (there are also leagues for women) gets most publicity and broadcast coverage, other summer sports have more participants, most notably lawn bowls. Golf is very popular and, compared with many other countries, cheap; municipal and club courses abound in the cities and towns, and many smaller settlements and country areas have at least a nine-hole course. It is popular throughout all social levels, and has less of the 'middle class' connotations that it carries in other countries. (There is by no means always a bar at the 'nineteenth hole'!) And a vast range of other sports, games, and activities attract smaller groups; team marching is popular among young girls, for example, another 'military pastime'. Indoors basketball is popular, and squash is gaining many adherents annually.

HOLIDAYS AND WEEKENDS

Most employed New Zealanders get all of both Saturday and Sunday free from work, which, since church attendances are generally small, gives a two-day weekend break for sport, hobbies and other leisure activities. Most employees also get three weeks of annual paid holiday; many Arbitration Court awards give two plus an extra for long-service employees, but in effect most get the third. There are also ten public holidays, including two each at Christmas and New Year. Only Anzac Day (April 17) and the Queen's Birthday (the first Monday in June) are outside the summer months. The National Day is 6 February—the date of the Treaty of Waitangi's signing—and each 'province' also has its own holiday. Annual holidays are taken mostly from Christmas until the end of January's second week (although the best weather is commonly in February); during that period New Zealand is in many respects closed, just as it is during weekends.

For many people, the holiday period is when they become members of the 'outdoor society'. Not many go to either boarding houses (of which there are few) or hotels. (There are relatively few of the latter except in the big cities and the main resorts for international tourists.) There is a dense network of motels, however, at which guests cook for themselves in their rooms—few motels have a restaurant attached. Motels are popular with people on touring holidays, but many more make their own provision. For some, this is their second home or 'bach' (the term 'crib' is used in the 'Scottish' areas of the South Island). There are 35,000 of these (one for every twenty households); some are in isolated spots, but most cluster on an attractive coastal stretch, at the mouth of a good fishing river, or on the shores of a lake. Many are not far from the owners' homes, so some members may commute from them for part of the summer. The early ones are small weatherboard huts and cottages, but many are now substantially built; they are often left unoccupied for several months, suggestive of a trusting society.

Caravans and/or canvas are widely used by the non-bach owners. Again, many go only a few miles from home to a large camp ground which has many amenities plus a wide range of organised activities during the main holiday periods. The Bay of Islands, the Coromandel Peninsula, Tauranga, Lake Taupo, Napier, Nelson, Golden Bay, Westport, the Christchurch area, Timaru and Lakes Wanaka and Wakatipu are the most popular locations. As elsewhere in the world, many return to the same place every year; in fact, a large proportion of New Zealanders have not visited many parts of their country, especially the 'other island', although the car ferries are frequently fully booked for the holiday season months in advance. More, it often seems, save up for the 'overseas trip'—which may be a working holiday and is usually to either Sydney or London; Fiji is becoming increasingly popular for holidays.

New Zealand has a great holiday splurge at one time of the year, which has given rise to the apocryphal story of the traveller who replied when asked if he had visited the country, 'O yes, but it was closed that week.' This concentration of the holiday season into three or four weeks has several disadvantages. Newspapers tend to be thin, since virtually no local news is being generated; TV shows only sport and 'repeats'—indeed current affairs programmes do not restart until March. The coincidence of Christmas and mid-summer means that, unlike the northern hemisphere, there is no mid-winter break in work.

HORSE-RACING AND GAMBLING

Horse-racing continues throughout the year, and Sunday is the only time when it can be guaranteed that there is no meeting. The 'sport' is closely controlled by government licences, and a total of 404 days racing is allowed—271 for flat racing and steeplechase/hurdles, 133 for trotting. A large number of the trotting meetings are held under floodlights.

The basic rationale of horse-racing for most people is the associated gambling: this, too, is closely controlled. A referendum in 1949 overwhelmingly supported plans for the installation of a Totalisator Agency Board, and the outlawing of all private bookmakers. Off-course TAB facilities are widely available in towns and suburbs, and New Zealanders are avid users. Some $175 million are 'invested' each year at present (the minimum stake is $1): $140 million are returned to the punters. Gambling on the horses or the 'trots' is widespread throughout society; among university students, for example, there are many 'investors' and followers of form. The proceeds of their failures are divided equally between the government and the TAB/racing clubs, with a small sum going to racecourse improvements.

Horse-racing generates much employment and activity in associated industries. Perhaps most apparent is the race commentator whose stereotyped monotone, frequently culminating in 'I won't name it', is relayed at the course and on both radio and TV. Adherents are well catered for in the daily (often two pages) and Sunday newspapers, in addition to specialist publications. And the breeding and training of livestock is a large industry. There are large stables in several parts of the country, but there are also many small owners, especially in trotting; the aerial approach to Christchurch from the south shows the large number of private training circuits. New Zealand livestock has a high international reputation, producing the winners of many of Australia's big races and gaining considerable overseas exchange, from the United States as well as Australia. (Cardigan Bay, a New Zealand-bred horse, was the first to win $1 million in stake money on the American trotting circuit, a feat recognised by a special stamp and a hero's return to New Zealand for retirement.)

Betting on horse-races is the most important form of gambling, although it rarely produces big winnings. (Jackpots, won only when the victor of every race at a meeting is picked and which accumulate around a club's circuit, are now limited in size.) There are no football pools or similar betting schemes, but there is plenty of small-scale gambling. Weekly 'housie' (bingo) sessions are very common, in taverns and working-men's clubs particularly, as money-raisers for sporting and other clubs; the city of Wanganui, with about 30,000 residents, presently has about 150 regular licensed housie sessions. And raffles are ubiquitous.

For a long time, purchase of tickets in overseas lotteries, particularly the Australian one known as *Tatts*, was frequently indulged. Such investment was illegal, but almost invariably condoned, as when the Rector of Canterbury University College —an economist—won, on Tatts, embarrassingly just before the graduation ceremony which he entered to the strains of *The Man who broke the Bank at Monte Carlo*. This was euphemistically known as victory in an 'overseas consultation'. Tickets were sold fairly widely; a few tobacconists still discreetly advertise 'We post to Hobart'.

In 1962, the New Zealand 'Golden Kiwi' lottery was introduced. Tickets cost 50 cents, and the lottery closes and is drawn as soon as 250,000 are sold; at present it is drawn about once every eight days. On average each New Zealander buys three tickets per year. The main prize is $24,000. There is also a 'Mammoth Golden Kiwi' lottery, whose tickets cost $2, and which is also drawn after 250,000 are sold; at present about twice a year. Both lotteries return just over half of their income in prizes: the remainder is distributed to various bodies and organisations, notably those involved with youth and aged citizens, sporting and cultural bodies, and medical research. The lotteries have recently been declining in popularity, and the distributed profits (about $1.5 million) are now only three-quarters of their peak value.

LIQUOR AND THE PUB

The New Zealander's great thirst for beer has already been demonstrated. As important as how much he or she drinks, however, is the drinking environment; the local system of quenching the thirst has many idiosyncracies. Very significant, too, are the effects of increasing consumption of alcohol on many aspects of social life.

The first alcohol, and the first problems, were introduced by the first pakeha and the early settlements in the Bay of Islands were notorious for the consumption of booze and the consequent behaviour, particularly of the Maori people whose capacity for alcohol in no way matched that of the hardened seamen. The gold rush period was another time of intense debauchery, when to be a publican was undoubtedly a much easier way to wealth than to be a digger. Bars were plentiful; Hokitika, a town of a few thousand residents, had eighty-four bars along its 'main street' in 1886.

Problems created by alcohol have characterised several pioneer societies, New Zealand among them, and a usual reaction has been a strong movement for prohibition. The New Zealand Alliance for the Abolition of the Liquor Traffic was formed in 1886, on the main policy issue that the public should have the right to determine, by secret ballot, whether the liquor trade should be allowed to continue. By 1894, it had achieved a poll in which each electoral district could decide whether licences in the area should be reduced or rescinded; in 1896 this 'local option' poll was added to the triennial general election, and it is still there. Several districts—notably Auckland and Wellington suburbs and much of the southern South Island—voted themselves 'dry'; four have never restored licences—two in Auckland and two in Wellington.

The peaks of success for the Alliance came in the first two decades of the twentieth century. By 1908, prohibition had a majority in the country as a whole, but a sixty per cent vote was needed for success, and there was pressure for a national referendum on the subject. This was held in 1914; prohibition just lost. And then in 1917, a board investigating the country's efficiency relative to the war effort reported that the liquor trade had harmful effects and that there should be a referendum on the straight issue of continuance or national prohibition with compensation (estimated at £4.5 million). This was held in April 1919. On the day, prohibition won by 14,000 votes out of 478,000, but four out of every five soldiers overseas voted for continuance, which finally won by 10,000. Since then, the prohibition cause has steadily lost ground.

Throughout the struggle, vested interests have opposed those of the Alliance. The most notable has been the brewing lobby, one of the strongest in the corridors of power. (It reputedly makes large contributions to both political parties.) This has gained in strength with concentration of both breweries and hotels (tied houses) into two main groups: Dominion Breweries and New Zealand Breweries. It and the other lobbies have successfully outmanoeuvred the prohibition cause; to be carried, for example, prohibition required a three-fifths majority, except at the 1919 poll, and since 1919 the prohibition vote has been split in the triennial referendum by the inclusion of a third possibility: the voter now chooses between 'National Continuance', 'National Prohibition', and 'State Purchase and Control'. (The latter is not a cause espoused by the Labour Party.) The Alliance's only successes were the overall reduction in the number of licences, the local options to go 'dry' and, in 1917, the introduction of six o'clock closing each night for all bars.

For several decades in this century, New Zealand—along with most Australian states—has experienced drinking conditions brought about by the complex licensing legislation introduced to counter the extreme views of the Alliance. In total, these conditions have had a number of effects on drinking habits. Most notorious was the 'six o'clock swill', the mass consumption of beer by workers in the hour after work, followed by a semi-drunken journey home, increasingly by car. To cater for this, mass consumption methods were devised. Draught beer is delivered to the pubs in large tankers and transferred to storage tanks under pressure through large hoses (in almost exactly the same way as petrol is delivered to service stations). It is served through pistol-like nozzles at the end of plastic hoses; the usual receptacle is a jug, containing about 32 fluid ounces. During the 'swill', drinking was fast, and on an empty stomach. Bars were large and built for this 'peak hour trade'; it was standing-room and males only.

One area of the country has consistently deviated from this national pattern; the relatively isolated West Coast of the South Island. There illegal 'after-hours' service has been condoned by the police (so small in numbers that they seem to have little alternative); occasional raids are invariably preceded by a tip-off. Bars would close between six and seven so that men went home for a meal; but after that, and on Sundays, back-door entry was possible. But drunkenness has always been much rarer there, with the numerous small bars encouraging 'social drinking'.

A consequence of the local option polls and the general refusal to grant new licences is that there are very few suburban bars; most licences are concentrated in the central city areas, close to workplaces. Many suburban residents are several miles from a bar, and must drive there. In recent years, the breweries have been successfully transferring licences within districts and opening suburban taverns to replace city-centre hotels (they are also closing some rural hotels to obtain transferable licences). But the suburban tavern is frequently a 'beer-barn', continuing the old mass-consumption methods and drawing most of its customers in their own cars; the taverns are usually set in large car parks. Drinking and driving is thus encouraged. Many taverns become very full, especially on Friday and Saturday nights, and there is now a ten o'clock swill—engendered, many believe, by the continued use of large capacity jugs which are filled, perhaps more than one per person, just before closing time. Fights are common; car parks are frequently littered with broken glass; drunken driving accidents are increasing; late night violent crimes are rapidly increasing in number at present.

Six o'clock closing encouraged home drinking. Quart bottles can be bought by the dozen at wholesale prices, and bags of them are still carried away by many. As common are half-gallon flagons of draught beer (half-Gs), filled under pressure. Bottle-store sales for off-premises consumption are still high, as is consumption at home, at parties, and at public events such as rugby and cricket matches. (The 1974 Australian series of cricket tests produced several problems with drunken spectators.)

Attitudes to liquor and its sale have changed in the last few decades, and especially since 1967. Most of the 'dry' districts have now voted for restoration; many of them then choosing that the licences should be allotted to locally controlled Licensing Trusts rather than to the breweries. And in 1967, a referendum decided by a two-to-one majority for later opening hours and 10 o'clock closing was immediately introduced—to be succeeded by a barmen's strike! (All pubs are still closed on Sunday.) Standards of hotels and taverns are closely controlled by the Licensing Control Commission (taverns are new, previously all hotels had to provide accommodation), and many licensed restaurants are now being opened. There is a strong Working Men's Club movement also, with excellent facilities and a wide range of social activities, as well as cheap beer.

But still there is an alcohol problem, and the vote for prohibition is still there (about fifteen per cent in 1972). Many bars are now much more comfortable, and more women are seen in them. The six o'clock tradition still lingers, especially on Fridays: often it produces heavy drinking throughout the evening. Drunkenness as a crime is becoming less frequent, but many people in the streets are clearly suffering the effects of drink. Indeed, the ability to consume great quantities of beer is a part of the male ethos, at all levels of society; even to vomit publicly (chundering is the local term) is frequently applauded, as part of a weird *machismo* cult. And there is an increasingly strong desire, it seems, to break glass bottles, and frequently to use them as offensive weapons. Of course, most take their bottles home, and the 'bottle drive'—collecting empties to gain the deposit on them— is a frequent method of raising money for several organisations; often they are piled at front gates on a Saturday morning, await- ing collection.

SOCIAL LIFE

A suburban society is commonly believed to be full of stresses and tensions, especially among the full-time housewives who are its permanent residents, and for the teenagers who can find little to do in the evenings. Both are problem groups in some areas, especially the large State housing estates where community facilities are few and gang warfare, commonly associated with motor-cycles ('bikies'), is increasing in its intensity. But for a wide spectrum of the total society there is a varied social life, much of it of the 'self-help' variety based on social, cultural, and sporting bodies. Indeed, New Zealand's suburban society could alternatively be described as a 'committed committee society'. A large proportion of people is engaged in some organising task (although a majority probably rarely leave the TV set); this gives a little bit of community responsibility to the individual— perhaps powerlessness is as corrupting an influence as power, so that the involvement is a positive aspect of social organisation. Cultural and craft activities—spinning and potting, for example —are extremely popular, in the home and at evening classes.

Daytime social life is organised around the teacup and coffee table; bridge and whist are probably less common than in other societies. Evenings may be taken up with hobbies and pastimes, in which people from various walks of life mix together as a result of their absorption with the chosen interest. Social snobbery is less apparent in New Zealand than in many other countries; there are groups, of course, based on either inherited status, such as being descendants of the first four ships that brought settlers to Canterbury, or attendance at a school with a strong old-boys or old-girls net (this is common of some of the older State, single- sex foundations as well as the private schools). Lions, Jaycees, Rotary and similar organisations are widespread and very active.

Much social activity is based on food and drink. A housewife may spend her day at the stove preparing cakes for a stall to raise money for a new school library, or bottling fruit to sell at a church fair. Or the food may be for a party that evening. The typical New Zealand party centres around the half-G and sweet sherry bottle; the invitation probably said 'BYOG' (bring your own grog) and 'Ladies a plate' (preferably with savoury or confectionery; common is the pavlova, a meringue topped with cream and chinese gooseberries). The stereotyped New Zealand party—at which the food is served late, as a buffet—has the men at one end of the room drinking beer and discussing sport and the women at the other, sipping soft drinks and chatting about babies and bottling. The story dies hard; it is not entirely false, but increasingly the division of labour and life between sexes is becoming less clear-cut and this is reflected in social behaviour.

Eating out at commercial establishments is not common, though the habit is increasing with the liberalisation of laws on licensed restaurants. The big cities, Auckland in particular, now have a range of good restaurants and night clubs; strip-joints are so far new and few. But the ubiquitous food establishment is the fish-and-chip shop, whose partially cooked wares are reheated in individual portions as ordered, to be taken away. Steak and fried chicken bars are increasing in number, as American chains move in to the main cities, but the 'greasy shop' still is the major source of out-of-the-home food.

CULTURAL ACTIVITIES AND THE PERFORMING ARTS

Professional performing arts are not strong in New Zealand, nor are the visual arts. For a small population, dispersed among several main settlements and remote from the cultural main-streams of the world, this is probably not surprising. Only Auckland can offer large audiences on sufficient nights to make many shows commercially viable, which means that in many instances the rest of New Zealand is a 'cultural desert'. And, as a consequence of this, the locally-produced performer soon finds that he or she must go overseas to find stimulus and sufficient work. Professional theatre companies have a typical history of early promise and rapid demise. There is no film industry, though there is much local talent as displayed by the makers of *This is New Zealand* for Expo 70 in Japan, while ballet and opera have never had long-lived successful companies.

Apart from the size problem, the absence of facilities is another reason for the near-absence of the professional theatre. Indeed, the opening of Christchurch's Town Hall complex in 1972 has made a great difference to the type and range of cultural entertainment offered there, involving international artists (albeit 'popular' if not 'pop') who can be flown in for a one or two-night stand. Prices are high but are paid, perhaps partly as a novelty because they give many New Zealanders a chance to see in person artists whom television has brought to their living rooms during the last decade.

To counter the lack of professional theatre, amateur companies and productions abound—concentrating on the 'classics' and proven favourites. These are probably on the decline in the larger cities, faced with the twin competition of TV and the commercial visitors. But the 'self-help' tradition continues, frequently at a high standard, assisted by immigrants and by locals—such as Dame Ngaio Marsh in Christchurch—who have spent long periods overseas.

Many types of music have a strong following in New Zealand; most of them involve amateur performers. Choral music is particularly strong, especially in Christchurch which has two large choirs of international renown, one of which has toured Britain. In the field of instrumental music, New Zealand is strongest in brass bands, and both its National Band and the Army Band have won much applause on recent world tours, as well as in the world TV coverage of the 1974 Commonwealth Games at Christchurch. Brass band competitions are strongly supported, especially in the South Island, as are pipe bands. Instrumental music is widely taught—in schools, by private teachers, and in Saturday morning civic classes—but there are few orchestras. The National Youth Orchestra is formed for a short season each summer and there is a National Symphony Orchestra—a full-time professional organisation—based in Wellington and supported by the Broadcasting Corporation.

The local scene initially offered artists two major subjects; the landscape and the native peoples. The latter were treated sympathetically, with emphasis on their unique features, notably the facial tattoos whose portrayal was perhaps best achieved by Charles Goldie. The landscape was depicted either topographically, usually in water colours, providing an accurate record of New Zealand's scenery, or else romantically, in the tradition of European landscape painting. Only in the last few decades has a more idiomatic New Zealand form developed, emphasising such themes as the vast openness of the inland basins of the South Island or the matriarchal dominance of the colonial society.

In architecture, the various bungalow styles of the nineteenth and early twentieth centuries were all of alien origin, with emphases on the verandah and the venetian blind to protect wellwindowed rooms from the summer sun. Little or no attempt was made to adapt and develop the traditional Maori building form, though some elements of its high-gabled morphology are evident in the work of the present generation of architects who are avidly seeking a separate identity.

Nurturing of a national cultural identity requires widespread education and display. Many aspects of the country's past are very effectively presented in the museums of the main cities, and in smaller specialised collections in other towns. Maori and other Polynesian artifacts are frequently emphasised, though there are examples of other cultures and of New Zealand's European culture: the Canterbury Museum, for example, has a reconstruction of a colonial period street. Art galleries are in general less well-catered for, and are not well-endowed; there is a growing interest, however, and an increasing number of private galleries.

Public support for the arts is provided by the Queen Elizabeth II Arts Council, which disburses grants to organisations involved in music, the theatrical arts, and the visual arts. It is at present concerned particularly with ensuring cultural development in all parts of the country. A third of its income comes from the Golden Kiwi lottery profits, the remainder from a direct government grant. In addition, there are private bequests providing, for example, annual prizes for paintings, and other institutions make notable contributions. The University of Canterbury supports a resident string quartet, which gives public concerts, for example, and the University of Otago offers three annual fellowships, one each in literature, music and painting. The New Zealand Historic Places Trust encourages an interest in aspects of the cultural heritage, and invests where possible in the upkeep of noteworthy buildings.

LITERATURE

Development of a New Zealand literature has been as slow and as difficult as that of other local art forms. Like them, it required the slow maturation of generations who considered themselves New Zealanders and who had relatively deep roots in its culture, rather than the interpretations of others brought up in different milieux. Meanwhile, those literary forms of the 'Old World' dominated the teaching of literature (even today, New Zealand literature is minimally taught in some of the country's universities), thereby perhaps inhibiting native growth. And, as with the other art forms, the few opportunities locally led writers like Katherine Mansfield to travel to Europe, both for the stimulus of a highly-developed literary world and for a culture where the pioneer demands of 'breaking in the country' and the consequent 'outdoor society' were weak. A large proportion of early books on New Zealand, therefore, were the accounts of short-term visitors.

Slowly however, a New Zealand literature has developed, though it is not clear just how widely it is read and appreciated. Auckland has produced a number of poets who have built on local and Pacific themes, though it is doubtful if the general population knows of more than one, 'Whim Wham', whose satirical, often cynical, verses have been syndicated on the leader pages of Saturday morning newspapers for many years now. Novelists, too, relate the New Zealand experience, perhaps none more powerfully for the years up to the 1930s depression than John A. Lee with his semi-autobiographical tales of a Dunedin lad's experiences of slums and 'borstals', of soldiering and 'swagging' (itinerant farm work), followed by his years as a rebel first within, and then when expelled from, the Labour Party. Often it is the small town and farming scene which dominates, as in much of the work of Janet Frame, Dan Davin, and Maurice Shadbolt. Increasingly, the urbanisation of New Zealand is being recognised in its literature, often emphasising the problems of assimilation to the city life, in particular for the Maori.

If New Zealand writers have problems finding publishers and audiences for their novels, short stories, and poems, there are two literary forms which they have no difficulty selling; the local history and the picture book. Examples of the former abound at the present time, as cities and boroughs, counties and districts, schools and churches, all are celebrating their centenaries and are marking these by the commissioning of special works, most of which publishers have no difficulty selling. The marketing of the picture book—usually with a short commentary—is even more secure, and New Zealanders seemingly never tire of buying expensive volumes of excellent pictures, albeit usually of the same features, mostly topographical rather than people-centred.

More general and scholarly books are less frequently published, largely because of the smallness of the market. The most widely read recent histories—K. Sinclair's *A History of New Zealand* and W. H. Oliver's *The Story of New Zealand*—were both published in overseas series, as were the general interpretative studies—W. J. Cameron's *New Zealand* and books of the same title by James and Margaret Rowe, and W. K. Jackson and J. Harré. The two main publishers attempt to provide outlets for New Zealand authors, however, and with liberalisation of high school curricula a larger market is opening up. Increasingly, too, New Zealanders are becoming book buyers, not only of Ngaio Marsh's detective novels but also the mildly salacious stories of Barry Crump; two recent best-sellers have been Austin Mitchell's satirical *The Half-Gallon, Quarter-Acre, Pavlova Paradise* and R. D. Muldoon's (the present leader of the National Party) autobiographical *The Rise and Fall of a Young Turk*.

THE MASS MEDIA

If New Zealand society is relatively philistine, with its emphasis on materialism and functionalism, its relatively low consumption of cultural items is probably counter-balanced by the high intake levels of what the mass media have to offer.

Thirty-six daily newspapers are published at present, nine of them in the morning; almost all have been published since the nineteenth century. There is no national paper but instead each of the four main cities has one morning and one evening paper which serves its hinterland. Widest circulation is achieved by the morning papers—the *New Zealand Herald* (Auckland), which sells more copies than the other three combined, *The Dominion* (Wellington), the *Christchurch Press*, and the *Otago Daily Times* (Dunedin)—because they can be widely distributed through the provinces during the night. The metropolitan evening papers have to compete with the afternoon issues of the small town journals, and so have more restricted hinterlands; nevertheless there is no real competition. Every one of the urban areas has a daily evening paper except Timaru, which has only a morning paper; Tauranga, New Plymouth, Wanganui, and Invercargill have both morning and evening offerings, as also does the relatively isolated Greymouth. Finally, there is a weekly paper serving local needs in more than sixty rural areas and small towns (some of them publish two or three times a week), and suburban areas of several large cities also have weekly 'throwaways', the total cost of which is met by advertising revenue. Dunedin, Wellington, and Auckland each have a Sunday paper.

New Zealand newspapers are all locally owned, though there is increasing concentration into a few hands; the News Media Ownership Act was quickly passed in 1964 to forestall a possible takeover of *The Dominion* by the London-based Thomson organisation. Local, even parochial, news tends to dominate the front pages, therefore, and local sentiment is especially strongly expressed on the sports pages. Nevertheless, there is good coverage of world news, usually two or three pages, even in the provincial dailies. Almost all of it comes from agencies and is transmitted by the New Zealand Press Association, which provides also most of the non-local New Zealand news, since, apart from a parliamentary reporter in Wellington, the papers have no staff outside their own town. Farming affairs gain wide coverage.

In their editorial policies, the dailies are universally conservative and tending to support the National Party—only the now-defunct *Grey River Argus* and the *Southern Cross* can be said to have wholeheartedly supported Labour. Nevertheless, the policies are usually fair to both parties, with a common tendency to allow the opposition a weekly column, in both national and local politics: occasionally they rather overrate their influence—as with the Hokitika leader in 1939 that began, 'We have repeatedly warned Herr Hitler . . .' and many editorials in the metropolitan morning papers concern international rather than national affairs. Current interest articles seem invariably to reflect the 'bad' side of an overseas country—whether the state of the British economy or race relations in American cities, thereby creating rather misleading stereotypes which tend to be widely held. The correspondence columns are usually lively, with a range of topics covered by interested readers led by regular writers, often sporting *noms de plume* such as 'Mother of Ten' or 'Disillusioned Nationalist'; letters are frequently referred to relevant public figures or businessmen for reply—even to the Prime Minister. (When he was Prime Minister, Sir Keith Holyoake was listed in the telephone directory and frequently answered the random caller.) A great advantage of the papers is the amount of informed detail they provide about local issues, and the frequent debate of these; the consequence is a well-informed and relatively active populace in such matters as town planning.

Apart from the newspapers, there is a wide range of regularly-produced specialist journals meeting the requirements of professionals and businessmen, tradesmen and sports enthusiasts, and religious interests. There are few general-appeal magazines, however. The *New Zealand Listener* reaches about one household in ten. Its main appeal for many is its complete listings of radio and TV programmes, but it contains the widest cover of current and social issues, and of reviews. It is produced by, but editorially independent of, the New Zealand Broadcasting Corporation. *New Zealand Truth* enters one in every four households, carrying a range of 'moralising' crusades and scandals and the *New Zealand Women's Weekly* enters one home in five. There are now local weekly-issue encyclopedias, dealing with topics such as *New Zealand's Heritage* and *New Zealand's Nature Heritage*, but most of these and other specialised publications are imported.

Some come from Australia, most from Britain and America; South Pacific editions of *Time, Newsweek,* and *Reader's Digest* circulate widely.

Journalism is being slowly replaced as a major vehicle of communication by the spoken and visual media, radio and television. The former was introduced in the mid-1920s by a private company. This was nationalised by Labour, and a government department developed a monopoly of radio services, with occasional unfortunate consequences in the possible political bias of their direction, as during certain election campaigns and the 1951 government/unions confrontation. It is now run by an independent New Zealand Broadcasting Corporation, which can be directed as to its policy, in writing, by the Cabinet Minister for Broadcasting. The Corporation acts as a censor, and is very responsive to public pressure; less so to government or 'professional' pressure.

The radio services of the NZBC comprise both the national and local networks. The main national network—the YA stations—carries the major news bulletins—including several daily from the British Broadcasting Corporation—and weather forecasts, and the more 'popular' programmes, covering both current affairs and general entertainment. It also carries the correspondence school programmes, and, in Wellington only, parliamentary debates. An alternative national network—the YC stations—provides more 'serious' programmes—music, plays, discussions—in the evenings, for the four main cities only. Some sports commentaries are carried on the YC but most are on the YA. Finally, the service runs more than twenty commercial or part-commercial services, on which popular music programmes dominate but which also carry items of local interest including 'phone-in, talk-back' shows compered by local personalities. (These are also a feature of the private stations; one show during 1974 was hosted by the leader of the opposition and another received a call from the prime minister.) The commercial stations operate in twenty-two different centres. Since 1970, private radio stations have been licensed, although one was previously operating as a private station from a ship moored in the Hauraki Gulf; popular music, talk-backs, and local news items characterise their operations.

Television services were initiated by the NZBC in 1960, to serve Auckland, and by 1962 Wellington, Christchurch and Dunedin were covered. A series of repeater stations ensures that most of the populated areas can now receive the service. (Some of these 'booster' stations are locally owned and operated.) More than a quarter of households had a set by 1964, and at present about eighty-five per cent have at least one. There is a single channel, which carries commercials on four days a week only (there is no sponsoring of individual programmes). Programmes are shown for 65 hours each week, all between the hours of 2 pm and 11 pm except for special outside broadcasts or late films at weekends.

Until 1971, there were four separate stations operating their own sequences of programmes. There was no national link allowing direct telecasts from one part of the country to another, and current affairs programmes had to be videotaped and flown to the transmitters, as had news items. As only one copy of each programme was purchased from overseas, each item of a serial, for example, was shown in different places in different weeks, much to the annoyance of the traveller. (When, in 1973, all stations were linked into a single programme, the Dunedin station had to run the popular British serial *Coronation Street* four times weekly for about a month in order to 'catch up' with the schedule for the twice-weekly showing.) New Zealand content is low; about seventy per cent is imported—almost all from Britain and the United States. 'Local' content is even less; each of the four stations provides its own nightly twenty-minute local news review, plus weekly children's and gardening programmes. National current affairs coverage is quite considerable. Colour was introduced in late 1973 (sets cost about $800), and 1975 saw the introduction of a two-channel network, with one of these based on Auckland and Christchurch and the other on Wellington and Dunedin. The network has been linked to overseas services by satellite since 1971, though this facility is used sparingly, mainly for sports events and news items; characteristically, it was first used to relay a horse race from Melbourne.

The rapid growth of television has paralleled, and undoubtedly helped produce, a significant decline in cinema numbers and patronage. Twenty-five years ago there were 600 cinemas, and the average New Zealander went to the cinema twenty-nine times each year, paying 15 cents admission. Today, the average number of attendances is only five, at a cost of 60 cents; there are about 200 cinemas operating, most of them only one-fifth full. Most of those closed were in suburbs or small towns, or were 'circuits' of several rural settlements that involved a series of four, five, even six 'one-night stands'. (There is only one circuit left.) Films reach New Zealand up to a year after their release in Britain or America (there is no local industry) and then usually play an extended season in the four main cities. Censorship is relatively strict compared with some countries, but is becoming less so: in 1967, the censor ruled that *Ulysses* could be shown to sexually segregated audiences only; in 1973, the Minister of Internal Affairs ruled that the film *Clockwork Orange* should not be censored. (Books are also subject to censorship— by the Indecent Publications Tribunal—but its rulings are few, and are rarely a cause of much contention.)

An overall impression of the mass media in New Zealand might be that they are bland, with very few extremes. The newspapers are far from scandalous or crusading (except for the Sundays) and faithfully reflect community attitudes. TV interviewers are in general 'kind' to their subjects, and detailed 'grillings' are generally resented; personalities are usually the local 'nice-guys'. In a small country, with a dispersed population, it is unlikely that anything more can be provided; in New Zealand's egalitarian and comfortable materialism, it is doubtful if anything more is required.

8

Hints for Visitors

For most Europeans and North Americans, New Zealand is not the place for a very brief visit, except perhaps as a stopover en route to or from Australia. The introduction of cheap air fare packages at the end of the 1960s made it possible for more people to go there, however, and increasing numbers are going to the islands, either to renew acquaintance with relatives and friends or to sample the beauties of the attractive countryside.

GETTING THERE

New Zealand is now off the beaten track of the world's main passenger liner routes, and there are few connections either to Europe (whether via Panama or via Australia and the Cape) or to North America. Auckland is the main port of call, with about fifty ships docking there each year, compared with twenty which carry passengers to and from Wellington and one or two to Christchurch's port at Lyttelton. The journeys to New Zealand ports are long, and for travellers from Europe invariably involve several weeks on end at sea without landfall.

Flying to New Zealand can also be a long and tedious trip, though modern jets have a high standard of comfort and service. From Europe, a number of airlines carry passengers across Asia to Sydney or Melbourne, from which three companies fly to all three of New Zealand's international airports. (Again, the most frequent service is to Auckland.) This trip can involve several intermediate stops between London and Australia, so many travellers prefer the alternative route via North America's west coast. Auckland can be reached from London with only two other touch-downs—at Los Angeles and Hawaii—and there is a variety of other services, from Vancouver, Seattle, and San Francisco as well as from cities further east in the United States, via Hawaii, Samoa, Fiji or Tahiti, to Auckland, Wellington and Christchurch.

Many travellers to New Zealand go there on cheap return tickets, which may not allow stopovers en route (the same applies to a number of the cheap single-direction fares). It is possible, however, to select airlines and routes which either allow one stopover (Los Angeles is the most common point) or are bound to provide overnight accommodation—usually in Sydney— because of the problems of making connections. But, even for those not constrained by these regulations, only the hardiest travellers will not benefit from one or more stopovers en route. The effects of long flights on most people's health are considerable, if only short-lived, and are exacerbated by the rapid changes of time. (Those crossing the Pacific will also undoubtedly be frustrated by the problems of understanding the operation of the International Date Line.) If one has only a limited period in New Zealand and finds it hard to sleep in the pressurised jet cabins— in which meals are frequent and films increasingly common— then it is best to stop for a night or two at a couple of places en route, catching up with sleep and arriving in New Zealand refreshed and ready to enjoy its welcome. A range of places offer comfortable accommodation, plus attractions to interest the short-term visitor: Los Angeles, with its many excellent cheap package tours to the delights of Disneyland; the tourists' Mecca of Hawaii, the quieter dignity of Tahiti or the duty-free islands of Fiji; the teeming island cities of Hong Kong or Singapore; the harbour grandeur of Sydney. And for those with longer to spend, they can fly to Tahiti via the strange landscapes of Easter Island, or to Sydney via Africa and the national parks.

Before departing from home, all visitors to New Zealand will have to obtain an entry permit, stamped in their passport. This will be a mere formality for most tourists, but must be arranged before airlines will agree to carry you. An international health certificate, indicating that you have been vaccinated against smallpox, is also necessary, and visitors from certain areas may be required to have other certificates, indicating vaccination against cholera, for example. On arrival, there are inspections not only by Customs and Immigration Officers, but also by those of the Department of Agriculture, who are ever-vigilant against the possible introduction of foot-and-mouth disease, one outbreak of which could completely destroy the country's economy. New Zealand currency can be obtained at all international entry points; it is not generally available in other countries, but this is unnecessary with the widespread use of travellers' cheques.

GETTING ON

Visitors may find that among New Zealanders, some Maori people are rather more reticent than their pakeha compatriots, but in general they will find their hosts friendly and easy-going. Most of them will probably have had little contact with overseas tourists. Like the inhabitants of most countries, they are keen to hear their homeland praised, but apart from favourable comparisons between it and the visitor's home, will probably be little interested in countries overseas. There is a widespread belief that 'Kiwis' ask visitors for their impressions of New Zealand immediately they meet them; the apocryphal, stereotyped answer is supposed to be 'great place to bring up kids' (which it is!). Outspoken critics, especially recent arrivals who broadcast their views in press, radio, or TV interviews, are, not surprisingly, rarely warmed to, for New Zealand is a cosy society which will not react kindly to outsiders attempting to analyse it, either 'objectively' or passionately.

Moving among New Zealanders, however, the visitors will encounter few problems. They will find their hosts efficient but rarely officious, helpful and friendly, hospitable and hearty, but not overbearing. They will not, however, find the obsequious provision of services characteristic of many Anglo-Saxon countries; they may be expected to carry their own cases, but they will never be expected to tip, either directly or by adding an unasked-for 'service charge' to the bill.

GETTING ABOUT

Having travelled a long way to get there, visitors to New Zealand will want to make the most of their stay and enjoy the particular attractions which the country has to offer. Few of these are in the sprawling main cities, though each is worth a brief visit. Auckland is increasingly a miniature Sydney or San Francisco, but the beauties of its eastern harbour should be sampled, travelling on the boats which ferry commuters from several Hauraki Gulf islands. At Wellington, visitors can look at the way a modern capital has been stacked onto the steep, fault-line cliffs, overlooking the superb harbour and the rough waters of Cook Strait. The 'garden city' of Christchurch has a quiet charm which is excellently sampled in local bus tours. Dunedin has a sterner, more solid exterior—reflecting its Scottish origin, again in a beautiful harbour setting.

But the main attractions are in the countryside. Most peculiar to New Zealand is the 'thermal wonderland' of the Rotorua area. Hot springs, geysers, fumeroles, boiling mud pools, wisps of smoke from the most unlikely of sources, and the smell of sulphur abound in the town and its hinterland. In Rotorua itself are the hot baths, the boiling mud and geysers at Whakarewarewa, the Maori villages of Ohinemuri and Whakarewarewa, complete with a training school in Maori crafts at the latter. (Souvenir shops abound; unfortunately, many of the 'carvings' offered are of plastic.) Outside the town are numerous trout-filled springs, the simmering, eerie calderas at Waimangu, the village of Te Wairoa which was buried during the 1886 eruption of Mt Tarawera, the vivid deep blue and green lakes set in an emerald green landscape, and the mighty pine forests of the Volcanic Plateau. Further south, one càn traverse the Desert Road, from the shores of Lake Taupo alongside the flanks of volcanic Mts Ngauruhoe, Ruapehu, and Tongariro.

Whereas in the North Island it is only the occasional volcanic cones which pierce the sky, the South Island has an almost unbroken chain of snow-covered peaks along its total length. Gem of this Alpine range is Mt Cook, at whose base is a hotel complex offering unparalleled views and a variety of mountain, bush and glacier walks. Regular air services land there, and a squadron of light ski-planes runs short trips from the glaciers, often crossing the divide to visit the glacial fringe of the West Coast. But the whole of the South Island high country can be described only as majestic, with the snow-covered peaks, the deep glacial valleys, the silent, tussock-covered basins, the serpentine lakes, and, of course, the ubiquitous sheep. Many areas are easily accessible on all-weather roads; the more hardy visitor may want to get deep into the tranquil beauty, however, on one of the guided walks over successions of mountain passes.

Away from these major scenic areas are many other attractive districts—indeed, very little of New Zealand's countryside is boring to travel through. Much of the sub-tropical coast of the north and east of the North Island, for example, provides beautiful countryside to be traversed at leisure. In the South Island, there are the soft coastal inlets of Marlborough and of Banks Peninsula, the golden beaches of Northwest Nelson, the wild and untidy grandeur of the West Coast, littered but not despoiled by the cast-offs of two mining eras, the tidiness of the Canterbury Plains, with their mountain backdrop, and the green of Southland. For the more active, the Bay of Islands and the Bay of Plenty offer superb deep-sea fishing. Good hunting can be found in most parts of the high country of either island.

Movement between the main cities is very easy in the frequent jet services, and all visitors should fly over at least some parts of New Zealand in order to appreciate the rugged grandeur of its backbone. But most journeys should be made on the ground. There are comfortable inter-city trains, with some services passing through otherwise fairly inaccessible country (such as the Raurimu Spiral (p 110), and the Waimakariri Gorge on the Christchurch–Greymouth route). Bus services into the remote areas are regular and reliable, if the roads often make them rather uncomfortable. But flexibility is desirable when touring. For short-term visitors, car hire is relatively cheap, while for those spending several months, it may be more economic to buy a car for the stay, particularly if mechanical advice ensures the reliability of your second-hand purchase. (Bargains are few, but values are usually held.) Journeys are often slow, for the roads are frequently narrow and twisting, so it is best to be conservative in route planning; almost everywhere passed through will provide something to enjoy.

Where to stay while touring New Zealand may be a problem unless the visitor is prepared to camp, along with many of his hosts. There is an expensive Tourist Hotel Corporation hotel at each of the major resorts, and the main cities each have a range of establishments varying in quality and price. Elsewhere, the choice is either a bedroom at a local 'pub' or else one of the, ubiquitous it seems, motels. The former provide meals; the latter have each room equipped for cooking and usually sell basic breakfast foods to guests. Most places have one eating establishment, though the choice will be limited and the menu basic (fish and chips, pie and chips, plus steak). There are few 'quality' eating places outside the main cities.

New Zealand climate is variable, so a range of clothing is needed, whatever the season of one's visit, and especially if the high country is to be explored. The only hazard is the sandfly, present in large numbers where bush and either river or coast are in close proximity. Sharks occasionally make forays into the coastal waters, but in any case swimming should be undertaken only where beaches are patrolled. Of the souvenirs, good Maori carvings are excellent, but for those with limited resources, a *punga* vase (made of fern) may be an attractive alternative.

Bibliography

A BOOK of this type is dependent on many sources for its factual statements. Students of New Zealand are excellently served by two publications of the Government Printer:
McLintock, A. H. (ed). *An Encyclopedia of New Zealand* (1966), and the annual *New Zealand Official Yearbook*, a thousand or more pages, packed with valuable information.

Historical:
Oliver, W. H. *The Story of New Zealand* (Faber, 1963)
Sinclair, K. *A History of New Zealand* (Penguin, 1969)

Welfare:
Sutch, W. B. *The Quest for Security in New Zealand* (OUP, 1966)
——.*Poverty and Progress* (Reed, 1969)

Pictorial:
Imber, W. & Cumberland, K. B. *Pacific Land Down Under* (Reed, 1973)

General:
McLeod, A. L. (ed). *The Pattern of New Zealand Culture* (OUP, 1968)
Mitchell, A. *The Half-Gallon, Quarter-Acre, Pavlova Paradise* (Whitcombe and Tombs, 1972)

Acknowledgements

My major debt in preparing this book is to the three million New Zealanders among whom I lived for seven-and-a-half years, and to my colleagues and friends at the University of Canterbury. Among them I would particularly thank Willie Smith, Peter Perry and Jane Soons. The persons most deserving of mention, however, are my wife Rita, both for her usual editorial skills and for her continuous support, and my children Christopher and Lucy.

All the photographs were provided by, and reproduced with the permission of, the New Zealand National Publicity Studios, Wellington, to whom I wish to express my thanks. Finally, I am grateful to Mr J. S. Frampton who drew the map, and to Mrs Joan Dunn for an excellent translation of my handwriting into a typescript.

Index

167